GOOD PRACTICE IN NURSERY MANAGEMENT

Second edition

Elizabeth Sadek • Jacqueline Sadek

First published in 1996 by:
Stanley Thornes (Publishers) Ltd

Second edition published in 2004 by:
Nelson Thornes Ltd
Delta Place
27 Bath Road
CHELTENHAM
GL53 7TH
United Kingdom

04 05 06 07 08 / 10 9 8 7 6 5 4 3 2 1

A catalogue record for this book is available from the British Library

ISBN 0 7487 7548 X

Page make-up by Acorn Bookwork Ltd, Salisbury, Wiltshire

Printed and bound in Spain by GraphyCems

CONTENTS

FOREWORD

I first came across this book in 1996 when I managed a 40-place day nursery. I felt after gaining my NNEB in 1977 and a 2-year break from working that I needed to update my knowledge in this ever-changing field. I had also decided to start the Advanced Diploma in Childcare and Education, so thought it would be a very useful resource. I have subsequently become a Development Worker in the Early Years and Childcare unit of the London Borough of Richmond upon Thames, an NVQ assessor and Early Years tutor.

Whenever I give professional advice I recommend *Good Practice in Nursery Management* to students, staff and nursery owners alike. The need for training in management and leadership skills is high on the agenda for partnership. High quality care is crucial towards ensuring that all children arrive at school ready to learn. It also provides parents with the confidence that their children are well cared for

The expansion in childcare has provided both exciting challenges and opportunities and enormous responsibilities. *Good Practice in Nursery Management* is a manual of business techniques, which are currently taught in leading business schools, presented from a viewpoint and translated into a context that will be familiar to every trained early-years worker. It is also a textbook, which provides a complete course for aspiring managers. Finally, it is a working guidebook for practising managers, showing how to comply with legislation and regulations, providing a checklist of key points to good practice, and simple forms and record sheets to put into immediate use.

With the publication of the second edition of *Good Practice in Nursery Management*, Elizabeth and Jacqueline Sadek provide us with a foundation to support a national nursery practice and eliminate variations in quality of provision. I trust that my second edition of *Good Practice in Nursery Management* will be as well used as my first, and will be found in many nurseries, schools, and colleges throughout the UK for many years to come.

Margaret Monori
Early Years Day Care & Childminder Provider Support Officer

PREFACE TO THE SECOND EDITION

When the first edition of this book appeared in 1996 there was hardly any published material available to support nursery managers in their complex roles. This is no longer the case.

However, from the publisher's collected intelligence gathered in preparation for this current edition, we have been surprised and gratified by the number of colleagues who continue to respond so favourably to *Good Practice in Nursery Management*. The many who claim they could not have weathered the storm of the Ofsted inspections without its support include many middle school and some fairly large corporate groups – the latter certainly a big surprise to us.

The publication of the First Edition coincided almost exactly with initial attempts by central government to fund this sector directly, with the 'voucher scheme' partially meeting the nursery costs of four-year-olds and later replaced, expanded and refined to include all pre-school children.

With the government funding came the curriculum demands, came the targets, came the quality control, came the quantifying, came the inspections, and, in the fullness of time, came the mandatory National Standards implemented for full day care in September 2001.

Following the government's intervention there is now a plethora of written work including books, publications, magazines, website helplines, all anxious to inform the nursery manager. As we work we are told by a BBC newsreader that early years nurseries are the largest and most rapidly growing type of small business in the UK.

So, in the Second Edition we find ourselves challenged not only to take account of the National Standards affecting all the developments in the sector but of all the national and local publications. In the meantime we are determined to remain sensitive to the needs of new managers not yet bloodied by the past eight years of unremitting change and to the need to maintain and update applied management theory. We are also extremely aware of the changes in training provision in the sector and the new demands of continued professional development – another function of the system of direct government funding.

In response to these challenges we have now reorganised the work into four discrete parts.

Part I
Three chapters dealing with the manager's role, and with the legislative details governing the provision of early years care and education.

Part II
Three chapters dealing with the management and organisational theories chosen to illustrate the task of the manager in this sector.

Part III
Three chapters dealing with administrative systems, staff recruitment, staff support and appraisal and development, and with accessing external training. This part also covers team building and conflict

Part IV
Two chapters dealing with the management aspects of bringing in the DPEE published curriculum and, finally, with the management of quality assurance systems.

WHAT'S ON THE CD-ROM

At the back of this book you will find a CD which contains over 60 editable sample documents which will enable you to develop practical and reliable systems for your workplace. It provides you with sample job descriptions, contracts and documents covering all aspects of nursery policy. You will find instructions on how to run the CD on the disk body itself. The contents of the CD are listed below:

Important note

These precedent documents may be suitable for use in certain cases but must be amended to suit individual circumstances. It is important to be aware that the level of skill required to amend a document may be equal to that required in drafting it, and that advice should in general be obtained from the appropriate offices at Ofsted or Early Years Development Partnership before attempting such amendments. The authors and publishers accept no responsibility for any loss occasioned to any person using or relying on any of the material in this publication.

INTRODUCTION

This book is about developing the skills and strategies needed to run a nursery in the current climate of corporate nurseries, Ofsted inspections and constant new demands on staff.

A general view exists that there is an 'art of management' lying rather uncomfortably alongside a 'science of management'. The nature of what is being managed rather decides which of these camps individual managers fall into. Managing a nursery is very different from managing a toy factory, even if they are both child-centred.

The 'science' part refers to the paper base of the manager's role: the accounts, the rotas and the book-work. The 'art', on the other hand, refers to the people base of the manager's role: liaison work, personnel functions and customer relations. Charles Handy in *The Gods of Management* (1992) says 'management of organisations is not a precise science but more of a creative and political process owing much to the prevailing culture and tradition in that place at that time'. In this respect, a nursery is no different from any other organisation.

When nursery staff are promoted to being managers it is usually because they are good at looking after children and, precisely because they are good at working with the children, they are also good at the art part of the management task. It is supposed that because they know their job with the children, they can manage other people who don't know that job so well, or who have not been doing it for so long. Fortunately, this supposition is not altogether unfounded and, by and large, the manager will be the most competent and skilled worker on the nursery staff.

The skills already developed to manage children transfer quite well to those needed to manage staff, and the strategies used to organise the children's lives and development do provide good background experience for the task of organising staff and supervising their development. There are other similarities that will emerge during discussion of management theories and the work of the manager.

Where the childcare manager may have limited experience is in the ever-increasing science part: the administrative work, the fees, the records and the registration. However, it is likely that in this day and age most nursery workers will have a good knowledge of computers – even if only for a child's developmental programme – and will be able to find help to develop administrative skills in this area. Further help may also be available from local sources, and most systems can readily be developed to meet the needs of small centres. Larger centres will be able to afford more administrative assistance.

Transferable skills are also available from such workaday activities as organising parents' meetings, fund-raising and outings. Expertise in pure 'business' type areas like marketing, book-keeping, managing the waiting list, writing the staff rota, external liaison and so forth can, and must be, developed or strategies to delegate these tasks devised. To help with this, a CD-Rom is included containing samples of the paper base of the nursery manager's task.

In our profession, the move from a childcare worker to nursery manager is not as dramatic as a similar shift in other professions – medicine or teaching, for example.

In being a childcare worker you have:

- team experience, including conflict management
- people experience
- experience of supervising students and volunteers
- experience of being 'in charge' (even if only in charge of very small people).

As a childcare worker you therefore do have a good start in management skills and these skills will stand by you in times of needs – so have confidence!

This book aims to:

- refine the skills you already hold
- outline the area of legal and other responsibilities of a nursery manager
- explore general management theories and identify where your skills fit into these theories
- provide activities and exercises designed to further develop the concepts discussed
- provide sample documentation for all areas of work.

The book is written as a textbook for students on management courses and as a guide book for working managers who have not had the benefit of specific training courses and may be seeking alternative recognition, such as NVQ at Level 4.

As a childcare worker you will be familiar with, and subscribe to, the underlying principles and assumptions that form the value base of childcare. These principles can be applied by:

- demonstrating a caring and considerate attitude towards children and parents
- recognising the crucial role that parents play, and working in partnership with them wherever possible
- meeting all aspects of children's development needs
- treating and valuing children as individuals
- enabling children to be directors of their own learning
- promoting equality of opportunity
- celebrating cultural diversity
- using language that is accessible and appropriate
- sharing information and liaising with parents and other professionals
- ensuring the health and safety of children and others.

The move from managing children to managing a centre will undoubtedly cause you some discomfort. You will sooner or later find your deeply held beliefs in conflict with the pressure of your job, i.e. you will experience *role conflict*. You will need to give a great deal of thought as to what exactly being a manager means and set this against the underlying principles inherent in your occupational background.

One dictionary definition of 'management' is 'the act of managing; administration; the skilful employment of means'. In this book we view management more as a sensible working pattern of support, intuition and reason, including systems and administration.

You, as a manager, need to give some thought to your own perspective of the role: your own style and your own ways of doing things. The parallel with childcare work is again evident because each manager, like each childcare worker, has his or her own individual way of working.

GOOD PRACTICE

The role of the manager is to:
- ensure that the children are given a quality service of care
- support and supervise the staff who deliver this service
- consult and respect the wishes of the children's parents/carers
- provide adequate resources in the nursery to enable the service to function
- set up a rich and stimulating environment in which the service can be delivered
- undertake external liaison and fulfil an ambassadorial function
- assume leadership in preparation for Ofsted inspections
- be a role model for staff and children.

While this may seem a tall order, remember that there is no single *right* way to achieve all this although (also like childcare) there are multiple *wrong* ways.

The aim of this book is to help you spot a wrong way before you travel too far along that path – or when that does happen, to encourage you to forgive yourself and to provide you with some suggestions about the return journey.

Elizabeth Sadek
Jacqueline Sadek
West London, March 2004

PART I

1 THE ROLE OF THE MANAGER IN EARLY YEARS PROVISION

What this chapter covers:
- responsibility of parents/carers
- implications of the parent–child relationship for the manager's role.

This chapter examines the context of the management task in early years: the complex legal and technical relationships that impinge on the manager in a childcare setting, whether daycare, play group, school or special care unit.

First among these complexities, and most significant, is the manager's relationship with the parent/carer and the child. Another is the relationship between the manager and the various agencies, inspectors and officials who take the overall responsibility for scrutinising and monitoring the provision of children's services in the UK. Last, but not least, is the relationship with and the management of staff.

Responsibility of parents/carers

In providing care for children it will help the manager to be absolutely clear about who the clients/customers are. Without a doubt, the clients or purchasers of our service are the parents/carers. Parents/carers after the 1989 Children Act are no longer perceived as having *rights* as such in respect of their child, or of having rights *over* their child. Parents now have *responsibilities* towards their child.

Where a child's parents were, or have been, married to each other at or after the time of the child's conception they each have parental responsibility. Otherwise the mother alone has parental responsibility unless the father acquires it by court order, i.e. by making a parental responsibilities agreement (not available before the 1989 Children Act).

It is the parent/carer's responsibility to ensure that the child is cared for. If, for any reason, parents are unable to carry out this responsibility then the responsibility will be assumed by the Director of Social Services, or by some other person identified by a legal agent and making a claim to take this responsibility – an aunt or grandparent, for instance, although it need not be a blood relative under the 1989 Children Act.

PARENTAL RESPONSIBILITIES

These are defined as 'all rights, duties, powers, responsibilities and authority which by law a parent of a child has in relation to the child:
- not to harm, neglect or abandon their child, i.e. care for/show interest in the child
- to give physical and moral protection to the child
- to be legally responsible for the child's actions.'

So the parent/carer has the responsibility to provide appropriate care for the child and will have individual views about what might be most appropriate. Under the 1989 Children Act this decision and responsibility is theirs and theirs alone. If they take guidance from experts, such as school or nursery staff, it is their choice to do so.

The parents' views on child rearing are therefore most important and, being practical, it is best for business that every step is taken to recognise and respect the heavy responsibility the parents carry.

In recognition of this, the 1989 Children Act determines that we should work with 'parents as partners' which, from a childcare point of view, seems a sensible arrangement. However, from a management point of view, a true partnership is not really an option as the parents are our *clients*. We are working *for* them and if we work *with* them it is in the best interests of working more competently *for them*.

Discussion between the nursery manager and the parents is vital

Parents, being the purchasers of the service we provide, are our clients/ employers and in management terms should be viewed in that light, i.e. we work for them to help them carry out their responsibility to their child. We seek to supply the particular type of care and education they demand for their child – particularly the pre-school child – or they will simply take their business and child elsewhere.

The appearance of the corporate nursery is evidence of the emergence of this parent power, as is the demand for educational input in nurseries. Parents no longer see care alone as being adequate for their child, and in this they are supported by the Qualifications and Curriculum Authority (QCA). The specially devised pre-school curriculum is part of current inspection processes.

It is incumbent on the centre to develop a care and educational programme that parents will find desirable and which also satisfies the developmental needs of the children and is approved of by the Office for Standards in Education inspection (Ofsted). The model must then be marketed to the clients (parents) and potential clients. This situation pertains whether the nursery is in the private, corporate or the public sector.

PURCHASER AND PROVIDER MODEL

Many local authorities have developed a purchaser–provider model of social services. This model means that they no longer run their own services – for the elderly, or special needs, or childcare. They see themselves as being purchasers and others as 'providers'.

The nursery is a provider and may negotiate a contract with Social Services to accept a set number of children. In this case, the authority will also take an interest and offer guidance on the services provided. They may also expect extended visits by parents to the nursery, some instruction of parents, staff attendance at case reviews and other similar additional services – all of which have cost implications for the nursery.

THE RIGHTS OF THE CHILD

Children represent a different challenge to management because while they are not the 'purchasers', they are the 'consumers' of the service. This is a fairly unique situation brought into sharp focus by the 1989 Children Act and made more interesting because under the United Nations (UN) Convention, ratified by the UK in 1991, children have *recognisable rights*.

These rights were identified by the UN Convention in a series of articles or statements. They are enormously significant for all childcare staff because during the period when such staff carry the parents' responsibility, they have the duty to guard the children's rights in the same way as their parents do at all times.

INTERNATIONAL RIGHTS OF THE CHILD

Children's international rights have had some recognition since the early part of the 20th century. In 1924 the League of Nations officially adopted the Declaration of the Rights of the Child. The League of Nations later became the UN and made a second Declaration of the Rights of the Child (1959). During the International Year of the Child (1979), Poland proposed a Convention on the Rights of the Child which was passed by the UN General Assembly in 1989.

The Convention is only binding on those countries, which, by signing, agree to ratify it and are prepared to meet its provisions and obligations. Until this time no test case has been brought to the UN. The UK government ratified this convention on 16 December 1991 following the 1989 Children Act, which reflects the Convention.

The Convention on the Rights of the Child exists to protect the right of the child in the community with other members of his or her group, to enjoy his or her culture, to profess and practise his or her own religion, or to use his or her own language.

Some of the sections of Article 3 are quoted in full below, since from a daycare viewpoint this is the most important part of the Convention.

'**Article 3**

(a) In all actions concerning children, whether undertaken by public or private social welfare institutions, courts of law, administrative authorities or legislative bodies, the best interest of the child shall be a primary consideration.

(b) States shall undertake to ensure the child such protection and care as is necessary for his or her well-being, taking into account the rights and duties of his or her parents, legal guardians, or other individuals legally responsible for him or her, and to this end, shall take all appropriate legislative measures.

(c) States shall ensure that the institutions, services and facilities responsible for the care or protecting of children shall conform with the standards established by competent authorities, particularly in areas of safety, health in the number ... of their staff as well as competent supervision.'

However, various other sections are also important for us to note.

Article 5 states the duty to respect the rights and responsibilities of parents and the wider family to provide guidance appropriate to the child's evolving capacities.

Article 12 states that children must have a right to express their views on all matters affecting them with 'the views of the child being given due weight in accordance with the age and maturity of the child'.

Article 14 has two important clauses:

(a) The child's right to freedom of thought, conscience and religion, subject to appropriate parental guidance and national law.

(b) The state shall respect the rights and duties of the parents and, when applicable, legal guardians, to provide direction to the child in the exercise of his or her right in a manner consistent with the evolving capacities of the child.

Article 30 states that in places in which ethnic, religious or linguistic minorities or persons of indigenous origin exist, a child belonging to such a minority or who is indigenous shall not be denied the right, in community with other members of his or her group, to enjoy and practise his or her own religion, or to use his or her own language.

Although the UK ratified the Convention an enactment was later introduced which endorses family cultural rights at the expense of children's rights. This reform was justified on the grounds that it secures parents' rights to determine their children's religious and cultural upbringing.

The reform means that children are now in danger of their rights being breached at the hands of their parents or at their parents' wishes. This is a complex area and has been examined only briefly here in the *context* of the manager's role.

Activity

Undertake a survey of the Early Years Development and Childcare Partnership (EYDCP) information services to discover whether recognition is given to the UN Convention on the Rights of the Child. This information can be obtained from the local authority Children's Information Service.

In the UK the 1989 Children Act brought together nearly all aspects of the law relating to children and took cognisance of their rights. It encompasses the UN convention. Under this Act, agencies are expected to give due consideration to a child's religious persuasion, racial origin, and cultural and linguistic background, whilst protecting children from suffering significant harm in accordance with the UN convention and the prevailing political climate.

SUMMARY OF THE MAIN PRINCIPLES OF THE 1989 CHILDREN ACT

- The welfare of the child is the paramount consideration in court proceedings.
- Wherever possible children should be brought up and cared for within their own families.
- Children should be safe and be protected by effective intervention if they are in danger.
- When dealing with children, courts should ensure that delay is avoided and may only make a court order if it positively benefits the child.

- Children should be kept informed about what is happening to them and should participate when decisions are made about their future.
- Parents continue to have parental responsibility for their children even when their children are no longer living with them.
- Parents with children in need should be helped to bring up their children themselves. This help should be provided as a service to the child and the family and should:
  - be agreed with parents
  - meet each child's identified needs
  - be appropriate to the child's race, culture, religion and language.

Activity
This activity is designed to develop understanding of the key relationships and the context of the childcare task.
(a) Discuss:
   who are the childcare customers?
   who are the childcare consumers?
(b) List the characteristics of a childcare customer.
(c) List the characteristics of a childcare consumer.

LOCAL AUTHORITY CHILDREN'S CHARTERS

Following the ratification of the UN Charter and the 1989 Children Act, many, but not all, local authorities devised and published a Children's Charter. Here is an extract from a fairly typical publication at the time.
- Children's welfare and their rights to a secure, healthy and happy childhood are paramount.
- The experiences children receive in their early years are critically important in terms of future development.
- Children are entitled to expect that all adults will respect, uphold and preserve their rights and ensure that their stated feelings and wishes are taken into account.
- Children should have the opportunity to make choices and develop a sense of responsibility for their own actions appropriate to their age.
- Children, parents and carers should not be discriminated against, particularly in relation to colour, race, religion, gender, disability, medical conditions or background.
- Parents should be recognised and respected as children's first and continuing educators.
- Parents and carers have the right to be consulted as partners in any decision-making process related to children in their care.

When Social Services relinquished the inspectoral role to Ofsted these charters became redundant and gave way to the National Standards.

Make sure you know where to get your hands on:

- a copy of the booklet on the International Rights of the Child.
- copies of the National Standards. (For the sake of simplicity in this text we will refer only to the Standards indicated for *full daycare*.)

Implications of the parent–child relationship for the manager's role

The nature of the legal relationships between parents and children impinges on the work of any school or early years centres and those who operate them. The younger and more dependent the child, the more sensitive the situation.

The children use, or consume, childcare services – they do not choose them for themselves nor do they meet the cost. They have rights that staff are legally bound to guard but no responsibilities towards staff in terms of financial remuneration.

The parents clearly hold the legal responsibility for their children. They choose the school or nursery and they fund the service. They do not enjoy the care personally; they do not grow through the education. They can judge whether they are getting value for money only from the pattern of their child's behaviour and the fleeting impressions they receive when

Parents' impressions of the nursery are clearly important

delivering, settling and collecting their children, and, for the more discerning, from studying the published Ofsted reports.

GOOD PRACTICE

It is vital that all staff fully understand the implications of the parent–child relationship. There are strong implications for staff development and staff supervision. The issues of responsibilities and rights have both philosophical and psychological aspects and deserve much further exploration in a team setting.

In the nursery
There is a need to develop procedures or systems which ensure that the role of the parents is always recognised and any breakdown in the system that guards the parent's role is signalled immediately to the manager so that remedial action can be taken. It is vital that the staff understand the context of their work.

See Sample 24 on the CD-Rom.

KEYS TO GOOD PRACTICE
- Parents must be welcomed in the nursery at all times.
- Parents must be kept informed of all aspects of the children's activities.
- Parents' role in their children's lives must be respected in all professional liaisons.
- Parents' noticeboard should display a copy of:
  - Ofsted reports
  - staff photos and qualifications
  - policies
  - the curriculum
  - menus.
- Children should be respected as individuals in the context of their race, culture and language.
- Children should be allowed to be directors of their own learning.
- All staff should be aware of the wider legal requirements of the centre and understand the context of their job.
- All staff should be familiar with the local authority regulations and the Children's Charter.
- All staff should be competent in fire drill procedures.

2 LEGISLATION RELATING TO EARLY YEARS PROVISION

> **What this chapter covers:**
> - overview of children's legislation
> - the 1989 Children Act
> - the 2000 Care Standards Act
> - 2001 Special Educational Needs and Disability Act
> - relevant additional legislation
> - registration requirements.
>
> It is the responsibility of the manager to be familiar with both local and national publications outlining relevant legislation.

Legislation relating to children in this country has a long and painful history. Every Act passed has been a knee-jerk reaction to some dreadful incident of abuse perpetrated against a child. Such incidents provoke public outcry and precipitate action on the part of outraged individuals or hastily formed pressure groups and culminate in a law change argued through Parliament by impassioned activists.

Overview of legislation relating to children

Early last century, the Barnardo Bill was the result of the death of a London orphan John Sommers, or 'Carrots' as he was known (his hair colouring being the only thing to single him out and ensure his absence caused comment).

The 1948 Act was the result of the death of Dennis O'Niell, one of a family of three children placed in foster care on a farm during wartime conditions who was forgotten by the agency's administration until he was found dead of abuse and neglect.

The 1974 Act was the result of the death of Maria Colwell, a little seven-year-old removed from a loving foster home only to die in the midst of her own family despite the involvement of every childcare agency in Brighton.

The 1989 Act was the result of the death of Jasmine Beckford and a series of similar preventable tragedies, as well as other widespread and much publicised incidents of child abuse.

On each of these tragic occasions the desire on the part of all the agencies has been to get it right, to make things better, to care for and protect the children. Recognition needs to be given to all the individuals who expended years of their lives and much energy on these attempts to keep the children safe, whatever the outcome and however minimal the success.

We will now look at some of the key legislation in more detail.

The 1989 Children Act

The will to educate and care for our children has apparently always been present in the UK. The 1989 Children Act, implemented in 1991, takes a much wider brief than any of its predecessors and was described by the then Lord Chancellor as 'the most comprehensive and far-reaching reform of childcare law which has come before parliament in living memory'. The Act was welcomed by most workers and theorists because it gave a legal impetus to changes already in fact taking place in the field – changes published by the National Children's Bureau and already accepted nationally as good practice.

The Care Standards Act 2000

The 1989 Children Act was followed by the Care Standards Act (2000), the National Standard for Under-eights Daycare and Childminding. There are fourteen standards itemised but it was not until September 2001 that National Standards became compulsory in the management of early years centres.

The standards are written as guidance for inspections by Ofsted and encompass the requirements of the Qualifications and Curriculum Authority (QCA). They are set out under the fourteen National Standards and two Annexes: one for Babies and children under 2 and one for Overnight care.

Each of the standards is followed by a 'focus' statement, which describes the key features of that standard for each type of provider. Standards for each criteria are grouped for convenience but are also numbered for reference back to the basic National Standards.

The last section for each standard explains what an Ofsted Child Care Inspector looks for and how they will make judgements when carrying out inspection visits.

The guidance is imperative in shaping all new applicants who wish to be the 'fit persons' and as they prepare for registration. Working through each standard and understanding what the inspector will look for will help applicants prepare for registration. The guidance is also invaluable for existing providers in getting to grips with the new National Standards before being inspected. The guidance should be used alongside the National Standards for each different type of provision.

Special Educational Needs and Disability Act 200

The 2001 Special Education Needs and Disability Act resulted in the Sl Code of Practice implemented in January 2002.

All early years providers in receipt of government funding must have a written SEN policy (see Sample 6 on the CD-Rom), devised in collaboration with the management group.

The head of the centre has day-to-day responsibility for provision for children with SEN and should work closely with the specially identified member of staff – the Special Educational Needs Co-ordinator (SENCO).

The SENCO is charged with working with parents and other professionals supporting other staff with SEN practice, and with ensuring that educational plans are in place and that background information is kept up to date. The manager must ensure that all staff are involved in the development of SEN policy and are involved in working with SEN children. The SENCO has responsibility for the day-to-day operation of the SEN policy.

Other relevant legislation

Laws relating to the welfare of children are not the only legislation of which nursery managers need to be aware. They must also give heed to the following (listed in reverse date order):

- Offices, Shops and Railway Premises Act (1963)
- Equal Pay Act (1970)
- Health and Safety at Work Act (1974) and Management of Health and Safety at Work Regulation (1992)
- Sex Discrimination Act (1975)
- Race Relations Act (1976)
- Food Safety Act 1990 and Food Safety Regulation (1995)
- Control of Substances Hazardous to Health (COSHH) (1999) (see Sample 13)
- Disabled Persons Act (1986)
- Food Safety Act (1990)
- Report of Injuries, Diseases and Dangerous Occurrences Regulations (RIDDOR) (1995).

This long list of legislation, however, does not dominate the life and work of a nursery in the same way as the 1989 Children Act does. These legislative controls are applied to all employers and do not have vocational content nor do they offer guidance in our professional task in the same way as the Children Act undoubtedly does.

GOOD PRACTICE

A sensible arrangement is to hold on file a copy of all the relevant parts of the above legislation to ensure a check can be made at any time and particularly in preparation for the Ofsted inspection. Relevant sections are available in the small booklet which is a summary of the 1989 Children Act prepared for daycare and available from the local authority Children's Information Service.

1974 HEALTH AND SAFETY AT WORK ACT

The 1974 Health and Safety at Work Act details necessary requirements and places duties on employers and employees in the promotion of health, safety and welfare of persons at work. The Act also extends to those not in the employ of the organisation, i.e. children, visitors, outside contractors etc.

Sections 7 and 8 of the Act are of particular relevance to employees and are reproduced below.

Section 7
It shall be the duty of every employee whilst at work
(a) to take reasonable care for the health and safety of himself/herself and of other persons who may be affected by his/her acts or omissions at work;
and
(b) as regarding duty or requirement imposed on his/her employer or any other person by or under any of the relevant statutory provisions, to co-operate with him/her as is necessary to enable that duty or requirement to be performed or complied with.

Section 8
No person shall intentionally or recklessly interfere with or misuse anything provided in the interests of health, safety or welfare in pursuance of any of the relevant statutory provisions.

Registration requirements

The registration and the annual inspection process is comprehensive and time consuming, requiring personal inspection of sites by:
- an Ofsted Inspector
- a Development Officer appointed by the local EYDCP
- the fire department
- the environmental health department
- the police, who check on staff working in the establishment including caretaking and maintenance staff.

Inevitably these procedures can be subject to delays. Police checking is one area where the response time can be slow, which means a delay between the application for – and the granting of – initial registration.

Police checks on staff mean that no unchecked person can be left unsupervised in the nursery. Some authorities also charge for police checks, which can be a financial drain on some nurseries. In this case, it is advisable to ask the member of staff to pay for the check and, assuming all is well and the colleague remains in the post for an agreed period of time, the cost can then be refunded.

LOCAL AUTHORITY AND EARLY YEARS DEVELOPMENT AND CHILDCARE PARTNERSHIP (EYDCP)

In many local authorities, pressure is likely to increase in the future because the number of applications for registration, or requests for guidance in setting up a childcare facility, is expected to rise for both economic and parenting reasons.

The registering authority supplies a standard form that asks for details such as space, staff, children's ages, opening hours, and so forth. Most Early Years Development and Childcare Partnerships will become involved in the registration process. They feel it is important to be able to support people wishing to register facilities throughout the setting-up process, with both advice and information and they have, generally speaking, appointed a Development Officer to liaise with prospective providers for that purpose.

THE FIRE AUTHORITY

The two main Acts on fire safety are the:
- 1947 Fire Services Act
- 1971 Fire Precautions Act as amended by the 1987 Fire Safety and Safety of Places of Sport Act.

The 1947 Fire Services Act requires fire authorities to give advice on fire safety when requested. This advice is available free of charge to any person or regulatory authority which requests it. Fire officers will inspect premises at the request of social services departments to advise on their suitability for the purposes of daycare. Social services departments should encourage daycare providers to approach their local fire brigade for advice on fire safety.

The 1971 Fire Precautions Act covers fire precautions in occupied premises and is administered by fire authorities. Under this Act all nurseries require a fire certificate, which will specify fire precautions such as:
- the means of escape
- fire-fighting equipment
- means of warning in the event of fire.

The fire brigade has to ensure that any statutory requirements made under the 1971 Fire Precautions Act are complied with.

GOOD PRACTICE

Fire drill procedures should be displayed and made accessible to all nursery users, parents, volunteers, students and staff. Regular fire drills should take place, particularly after the appointment of new staff or the arrival of new students. These events should be recorded appropriately (see Sample 11).

It is a general requirement attached to fire certificates that all people who work in buildings for which a fire certificate is required shall be given instruction and training to ensure that they understand the fire precautions and action to be taken in the event of fire. The training should include people on regular duties or shift duties working outside normal working hours, including all part-time staff, cleaners and so forth. These arrangements must take account of the special needs of anyone likely to be in the premises, e.g. anyone with a physical handicap.

Of course, sensible fire precautions and good housekeeping practices will reduce the possibility of having a fire and needing to evacuate the building.

3 DEVISING POLICIES AND PROCEDURES FOR EARLY YEARS PROVISION

> **What this chapter covers:**
> - relevant parts of the 1989 Children Act and the role of the manager
> - the Ofsted inspection
> - the ethos of the nursery
> - mission and policy
> - using Policy Statements to write procedures and develop nursery routines.

The aim of this chapter is to examine the effects of the 1989 Children Act and other legislation on the service and on the management role in childcare.

The 1989 Children Act and the National Standards have been a great support to workers keen to deliver quality childcare and have made explicit many of the practices that have long been considered desirable, e.g. working with parents as partners, allocating key workers, producing written policies and delivering a relevant curriculum.

In this chapter we suggest management strategies to bring in the policies recommended by the Act and considered desirable as good practice and reflected in the fourteen National Standards. This chapter is about developing routines (procedures) and looking at what they are, where they come from and how they affect the manager's role in the childcare service.

Relevant parts of the 1989 Children Act and the role of the manager

The relevant sections of the Act are Part II (Local Authority Support for Children) and Part X (Child Minding and Daycare for Young Children). The Act and all the associated regulations are very detailed.

GOOD PRACTICE

All nurseries should hold a copy of the National Standards and relevant sections of the Act so that reference can be made to them at any time.

The Acts deal with private disputes between parents about children, court orders and care proceedings as well as with daycare and fostering.

The primary aims are to protect children, to prevent family breakdown, and to ensure minimum standards in services for children and their families. As we have noted, many such services have to be registered and inspected, including daycare and childminding of the under-eights. The early years directorate of Ofsted is responsible for registering and ensuring that the standards are met in all of these.

The key principles emphasised throughout the 1989 Children Act are outlined below.

- *The primary concern.* The welfare of children must be the prime concern of workers and authorities.
- *The role of parents.* Parents have *responsibilities* towards their children – they do not have absolute rights as if children were possessions (this had never been explicitly stated until this Act).
- *Sharing care.* Workers and authorities should work in partnership with parents.
- *Children's individuality.* In the provision of services authorities must take into account each child's and family's racial origin, religious persuasion and cultural and linguistic background. (This is supported by the UN Convention.)
- *Disabilities.* Children with disabilities are specifically included within 'Children in need' as defined by the Act.

The sections most relevant to daycare and the manager's role are published in the 1989 Children Act, Guidance and Regulations, Volume 2, Chapters 4–9.

Part X Schedule 9 and 2 (Regulations and Guidance) of the 1989 Children Act places upon authorities duties and powers to ensure minimum standards of care for young children and to assist in the development of standards. Ofsted is required to keep a register and to inspect the premises of all persons who provide daycare for children under eight. The duty is to ensure only the *minimum* standard and, although this term is not clearly defined, it is generally agreed to be a standard that will keep the children safe, comfortable and engaged in the Foundation Stage curriculum.

THE OFSTED INSPECTION

To ensure the standards are being met, the authority must carry out an inspection and the nursery/centre must meet the expense of this inspection. It is carried out by the official inspector appointed to each region.

One of the side-effects of the Children Act and the appearance of the National Standards has been the rapid increase in inspection posts – providing welcome and excellent career opportunities for qualified experienced nursery staff. Many of the inspectors are progressed nursery workers especially retrained for the purpose.

It is useful to keep an updated file in the nursery of the legislation for use with parents and staff, and to hold on file the names of experts who are available as a resource to answer questions or clarify issues should they arise.

The ethos of the nursery

The primary task of the manager is to create and control the ethos of the nursery. One dictionary definition of 'ethos' is 'the characteristic spirit or disposition of an organisation' and this closely resembles what theorists call 'culture' (although ethos is a more appropriate vocational term).

The ethos of any childcare organisation can be measured by a range of performance indicators that tell us whether or not quality care is being provided for the children.

The ethos (or culture) of a centre is palpable to all users and visitors. Although difficult to define it is not difficult to identify, even on the basis of a very few visits.

For this reason it is vital that the ethos, like the culture in theoretical terms, is appropriate to the task of the centre and reflects the published policies and declared mission statement.

You will be able to form a fair idea of whether your nursery/centre has a good ethos, if you can answer 'yes' to the following questions.

- Are the children happy? (That is, are they engaged and functioning at their age-related developmental level, without undue noise, squabbling or minor injuries?)
- Does the environment ensure that every child is respected as an individual?
- Is the dignity and autonomy of the children respected?
- Does the environment promote enthusiasm for learning and skills acquisition?
- Does the environment encourage children to express themselves freely and to be spontaneous?
- Does the centre offer a stable learning and caring environment?
- Is self-confidence promoted in the children?
- Does the centre promote good health?
- Does the centre encourage sociability and co-operation?
- Does the centre treat everyone equally, irrespective of gender, race, religion or disability?
- Is cultural diversity fully expressed?
- Is the centre fully sensitive to family influences?
- Is the centre in harmony with the wider community within which it is situated?

Each of the above questions can be answered by a policy or by a procedure or by the mission statement, which is dealt with in the next section.

In the corporate nursery these questions will be answered in the organisation's published material. Nevertheless, it is the responsibility of the manager/nominated person to ensure that all staff embrace the published statements.

Mission and policy

The nursery manager must articulate and record a mission statement, policy statements and procedures, as well as creating other publicity material. The manager must set up a team or group to share in the work of producing these documents.

THE MISSION STATEMENT

A sensible mission statement is one that is useful to the parents and staff, and others involved in the centre, and is merely a succinct statement of the aims of the organisation. It is helpful to have the staff articulate exactly what the nursery is trying to do.

While such statements have been made by managers of many organisations for many years, it is only in very recent times – noticeably since the 1989 Children Act – that managers in childcare have joined their number.

Here are some examples of mission statements for different organisations.

'Our mission is to contribute to the increased performance and competitive advantage of UK organisations by establishing, through the Investors in People Standard, the framework for effective investment in training and development for all people to meet business needs.'

Investors in People UK Limited

'The centre works to ensure that the educational and social needs of the children will be identified and provided for with due care and

Writing a mission statement

attention and in such a manner as will offer a reliable service for working parents, seeking wherever possible to enhance the quality of the children's total experience of family life.'

Someplace Nursery Centre

'The Council will strive throughout its work to enable professional workers in children's care and education to gain access to training and assessment in order that they provide the highest quality service to children and families. The Council will also act as a focus for national standards in children's care and education.'

The Council for Awards in Children's Care and Education

An effective mission statement will:
- state clearly the purpose or intention of the organisation
- indicate an underlying value system
- be written in good and plain English
- be no less than 30 and no more than 100 words long
- be translated into the first languages of all of the users and perhaps other languages where appropriate.

All workers in an organisation – particularly in a childcare organisation – collectively own the philosophy contained in the mission statement, and own the policies that are the distillation of the beliefs and intentions it contains. The group who write the statements must therefore have all staff, or representatives of all staff, involved. The group actually writing the statement should be between three and eight in number.

It is the role of the nursery manager to convene, facilitate, chair and steer this working group. It is the leader's task to establish policies and procedures for quality care.

The first meeting of the writing group will set the tone for the many that must follow, and should be handled carefully to ensure that it is relaxed and informal. Staff will not give of their best unless they feel valued and well supported. In preparing for the meeting, the manager should make some notes of ideas for the nursery's mission, for example:

'To care for and educate the children of the employees of the Somewhere Biscuit Company, to meet the needs of the children, to reflect the wishes and satisfy the childcare needs of the parents and to facilitate the work of the Company.'

'To support mothers on drug rehabilitation programmes and assist them in the care of their children, offering training, guidance and support in the development of parenting skills for that purpose.'

'To provide a structured educational environment for the care of children of Anyplace Hospital staff, respectful of their role in that organisation, in such a manner as to reflect their cultural diversity and allow for their flexible work patterns.'

In the nursery

Provide samples of other mission statements for your writing group. Sample 1 on the CD-Rom may be used or you could ask other nurseries for copies of theirs. The local social services daycare advisor will also be pleased to assist you with other examples.

Provide writing materials (flip charts and markers are ideal) and also refreshments.

Using the samples the group should then brainstorm what they consider to be the mission of the organisation with which you are all involved and which you all know well, even if it has never been articulated or recorded in quite this way before. It may help to brainstorm key words or phrases first, and then build these into ideas of the mission.

From the material thus generated, a statement can be assembled and checked against the above criteria to ensure that it has all the necessary features. The mission statement should be constructed in such a way that it will remain unchanged over time – it should be general – and not need adjusting.

The mission statement can be used on all of your publicity material, on the staff publicity and on the parents' noticeboard.

See Sample 1 on the CD-Rom.

POLICIES

The 1989 Children Act and the National Standards call for *policies*.

Policies exist to protect the children, the parents and the staff and to ensure that everyone using the centre is absolutely clear about the way the organisation functions and about what to do at all times.

A policy is 'a course of action or administration recommended or adopted by an organisation'. It is an articulated explanation of the way that a nursery will approach an area of work within its culture. A policy is a collective agreed statement of beliefs.

There are four main policies demanded under the 1989 Children Act:
- Equal Opportunities Policy – Standard 9/10
- Parents as Partners Policy – Standard 12
- Health and Safety Policy – Standard 6/7/4
- Child Protection Policy – Standard 13.

When the demands of the Act were distilled by the Office for Standards in Education, fourteen National Standards emerged. Some of the Standards did not demand 'policies' but more stringent procedures that had been only 'good practice' before September 2001. It is necessary to understand the relationship between the Act and the fourteen Standards.

Activity
This activity is designed to develop skills in identifying policies. In groups:
- Read the questions about the nursery listed on page 19. Each question reflects one of the policies required by the Act.
- Consider each question in turn and write down for each one the policy to which it refers.

Examples of policies covering these areas can be found in Samples 2, 3, 4 and 5 on the CD-Rom.

However, alongside these essential policies, the Act reflected in the Standards strongly recommends adopting other policies where they are appropriate and desirable for the well-being of the nursery. Some common examples are:
- Acceptable Behaviour Policy – Standard 11
- Admissions Policy – Standard 7/10
- Child Collection Policy – Standard 13
- Curriculum Policy – Standard 3
- Exclusion Policy – Standard 7/10
- Fees Policy
- Food Policy – Standard 8
- Intimate Care Policy (staff protection)
- Key Worker Policy – Standard 2
- Language Policy – Standard 3
- Outings Policy – Standard 6
- Quality Control Policy – Standard 2/14.

- Settling In Policy – Standard 4
- Staff Training Policy – Standard 2
- Staffing Policy – Standard 1/2
- Volunteer Policy – Standard

Examples of such policies can be found in Samples 8–10, on the CD-Rom.

(A Quality Control Policy is not technically required by the Act but having one provides a useful management strategy for systematising, monitoring and revisiting policies, both demanded and voluntary, and this emerged in the National Standards as Standard 14 – see Chapter 11).

The nursery can add policies to reflect local needs or to identify a philosophy, e.g. for a special religious or ethnic group. Samples of standard formats for these policies are given on the CD-Rom (e.g. Sample 12).

Each policy statement underpins a number of procedures, as illustrated in the diagrams below. For example, the equal opportunities policy gives rise to procedures for admissions, staffing, training, curriculum planning, food and administration. These procedures, in turn, give rise to routines and to procedures.

Once you have prepared all your policies, keep them all in a ring binder. Label it well and have a copy available in the staff room and in the office. Ask staff to sign their contributions and to include the experience of devising these policies on their CVs. This work will be greatly assisted if the National Standards are used in conjunction with the 1989 Children Act as source material.

In the nursery

When preparing the mission statement and policy, it is a good idea to meet regularly at the same time and place to undertake the work in small bite-sized chunks. Start with the mission statement and the legally required policies and then move on to writing the regulations procedures that reflect the policies. Use the samples provided in the CD-Rom as the basis for your work.

See Samples 1–5, 8–10, 12, 48 and 49 on the CD-Rom.

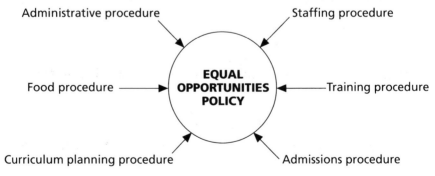

Procedures underpinned by equal opportunities policy

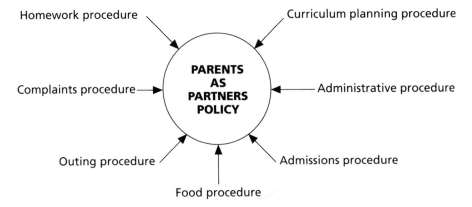

Procedures underpinned by parents as partners policy

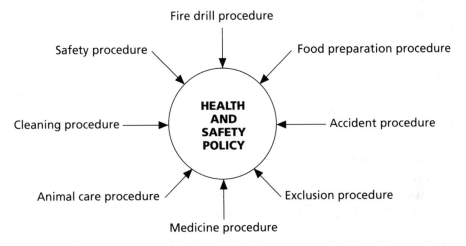

Procedures underpinned by health and safety policy

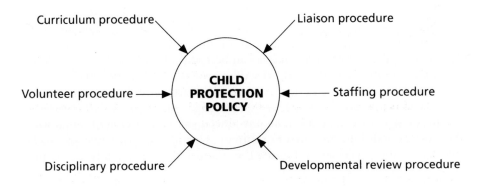

Procedures underpinned by child protection policy

One of the requirements of the Ofsted inspection is to follow regulations by having details listed of:

- Nominated person (Standard 1) – address and CV
- Names and addresses of:
  - all staff, vocational and others
  - anyone living in the premises
  - children registered
  - parents/carers of all children registered.

Ofsted Change Requirements are that:

- nurseries *must* notify Ofsted of *any* change of circumstances in the nursery
- a Complaints Procedure (against the nursery) must exist
- there must be a Procedure in the event of a child being lost (see Sample 26) or a parent failing to collect (see Sample 24)
- there should be registers for accidents/incidents/medicines (see Samples 27 and 28)
- there must be a Fire Drill (see Sample 11)
- a Risk Assessment must be carried out (see Sample 30)
- notification of Infectious Diseases must take place
- there should be First Aid box list
- there should be Nominated First Aid qualified staff member.

(See pages 59, 60, 61 of the *Guide to National Standards* (Ofsted, 2001).)

Using Policy Statements to write procedures and develop nursery routines

In the nursery

This exercise can be undertaken for each policy as it is written. The result will be a portfolio of procedures that will provide a system of articulating and maintaining the standards in the centre and among the staff.
  See Samples 14–20 inclusive on the CD-Rom.

If it is agreed to adopt a policy on quality control, this allows the development of a quality assurance system that will technically liberate the manager from constant checking up and will allow more time for the art of management. This same quality control technique can be used for all functions, vocational and administrative, e.g. to check off staff appraisals (see Chapter 11).

The policies, procedures and routines should be stored in a ring binder to allow for daily, weekly or monthly checking and, of course, inspection. A tick list or signature system can be introduced so that a system of monitoring the work is built into the nursery routines. This means that when you come to evaluate the processes and check the systems, there is already an existing structure – a routine.

The standard work in this field has been undertaken by the National Children's Bureau, which has produced an invaluable guide indicating good-quality childcare. This work can be used to provide simple guidelines so that each facility evaluates the quality of its service against a common set of criteria.

This would also help users in choosing the childcare appropriate to their needs, since it is currently difficult for the lay person to compare the quality of one nursery to that of another.

Ofsted inspection reports also appear on the Internet.

An understanding of what quality means helps the manager to regulate the quality of care provided and monitor the training given to care givers.

There are opportunities in this area for staff development and for job enhancement.

PROCEDURES TO PROTECT STAFF

The policy on Intimate Care has been devised to underpin the procedures for the toiletry and intimate care delivered to children. This policy is a form of staff protection.

KEYS TO GOOD PRACTICE
- Ensure that you and all your staff are aware of the National Standards and of the requirements of the 1989 Children Act. A pocket-sized volume covering all relevant areas is readily available and could be included in the staff induction programme.
- Make a copy of the questions on page 19 (taken from the European discussion document on quality) and ask yourself these questions with respect to each child attending your nursery.
- Ensure that the nursery has, as a minimum, the four policies required under the 1989 Children Act written down and displayed.
- Ensure that the nursery meets the other legal requirements which demand written displayed items, e.g. fire drill.
- Ensure that the nursery has a copy of the previous inspector's report.
- Ensure that the nursery has a copy of the National Standards.
- Ensure that the nursery has the website address for Ofsted.

PART II

4 MANAGEMENT THEORIES APPLIED TO EARLY YEARS PROVISION

> **What this chapter covers:**
> - the importance of research
> - research methodologies
> - organisational behaviour
> - structure, function and cultures in the work place as described by management theorists.

The aim of this chapter is to define *organisational behaviour* and to set the scene in childcare terms within that part of management theory generally referred to as 'structures, functions and cultures'.

Most of the theoretical research in this area has been undertaken in industrial and commercial settings – as part of the work of industrial psychologists or of organisational behaviour specialists (who are working from a psychological base). There has been very little direct management research undertaken in childcare settings. However, many industrial theoretical studies provide useful analytical tools for any manager. Briefly, we aim to examine how research is undertaken in this area and how much value we give research, before we look at how organisations/centres are arranged (structured) and how such arrangements can help or hinder the functioning of the centre, the jobs and the satisfaction of the staff. Clearly this will all have an impact on the quality of the service provided to customers (in this case, the parents/carers) and to consumers (in this case, the children).

The importance of research

WHAT EXACTLY DO WE MEAN BY 'THEORY'?

Throughout this text theories will be offered for consideration. It would therefore be helpful to be clear about what exactly a theory is – because even well-founded and accepted theories do not contain absolute truths and are not written in tablets of stone. A theory is simply an idea that one person (a theorist) has put forward to explain some observed phenomena, for example behaviour or patterns of behaviour in individuals in groups and in organisations.

CASE STUDY

The photocopier in an office will not give up its paper.

Someone has a theory (a) that the paper feeder is jammed. Evidence to support this theory is that in this individual's observation of other such occasions, the paper feeder was found to be jammed. Someone else has a theory (b) that the machine is switched off. Evidence to support this theory is also observation, i.e. that the plug is lying under the machine and is not plugged into the socket.

The weight of evidence for the second theory is irrefutable. Of course, the paper feeder may also be jammed, but that is not the most scientific explanation of the failure available at this point in time.

A theory is an idea offered to explain a phenomenon. It is not the theory as such but the evidence to support the theory that is the crucial element in the equation. Some theorists base their ideas on observation alone – Charles Darwin observed the world for years and came up with the 'Theory of Evolution'; Jean Piaget observed his own children over a much shorter period and came up with the 'Theory of Consistency'. A Greek philosopher named Archimedes got into a bath, observed the change in the water level and in a single instant leapt out shouting 'Eureka' and came up with the 'Theory of Displacement' (also known as Archimedes' Principle). He then, no doubt, spent long hours explaining the theory in terms of complicated mathematics. It was the mathematics as well as the bath that he offered as evidence. In using other people's theories it is vital to look at the evidence they produce to support the theory.

The idea or theory has to be expressed as a 'hypothesis' or prediction. For example:

'the photocopier will jam if you use the wrong type of paper'

or

'children will grow in confidence if given praise as a reward'.

Darwin's hypothesis was that organisms evolve towards specialisms by the principle of the survival of the fittest. To support his hypothesis he collected evidence. He travelled widely and by examining various animal species he conceived the notion of 'natural selection' which ensured the 'survival of the fittest'. By this he meant that the best-equipped individuals of any species, with all their strengths, survived long enough to reproduce and pass their genes to the next generation. He recorded his observations over many years until he was convinced that his evidence supported his theory and proved his hypothesis.

ORGANISATIONAL THEORY

The theories we will be using are, in essence, no different from this. They are sometimes called 'management theories' and sometimes 'organisation theories'. This latter term is the one we find to be the most useful.

In order to manage in an organisation it is valuable to be able to predict what might happen next, based on what is happening now or what happened yesterday – even if it happened to someone else. If you know what is likely to happen next you can organise yourself, your colleagues and staff to deal with that event.

Charles Handy (1992) tells us that organisation theory:

'helps one to explain the past which, in turn helps one to understand the future which leads to more influence over future events and to suffer less disturbances from the unexpected'.

It will help a manager to have some grasp of organisation theory. A theory is only of use if it is supported by evidence or if it is known to what extent the evidence supplied is weak or, indeed, non-existent. Theories with non-existent evidence are either:

(a) new theories not yet proven, or
(b) models or (paradigms) of reality – one person's, or group's, ideas of how the world is arranged.

An example of this second type of theory is R. Meredith Belbin's 'Theory of Team Roles' (Belbin, 1981), which is discussed in Chapter 8.

Paradigms or *models* are also often used in managerial studies and can be of great service when analysing a new situation.

A good example of this is McKinsey's 'seven 'S's, which is one way of diagrammatically representing the role and tasks of the manager. This model is particularly pertinent in childcare because shared values underpin our work just as they do in McKinsey's model. The model aims to illustrate the variables that managers must deal with when planning their work. It is organised in seven 'S's for easy recall. You will see that the listed areas of concern here are similar to the areas we will discuss:

■ shared values
■ staff support and motivation
■ skills needed for the childcare task
■ strategies – the plans we make for areas of the work
■ structure – of the nursery: what makes it work
■ systems – for care of records and for planning
■ style – the leadership style that is most appropriate for childcare.

Models and weaker evidence theories may be used and quoted and may be very helpful to managers.

However, these theories are unlike the 'Theory of Gravity', for example, which embodies an absolute truth and will predict results accurately every time – every object thrown up will come down again at some time attracted by the earth's gravitational pull. The evidence for the 'Theory of Gravity' is irrefutable – it can be proved mathematically, by scientific experiment and can be explained by the rational laws of nature.

The evidence for Darwin's 'Theory of Evolution' is not so strong. It is based entirely on observation of natural phenomena and is explained by an

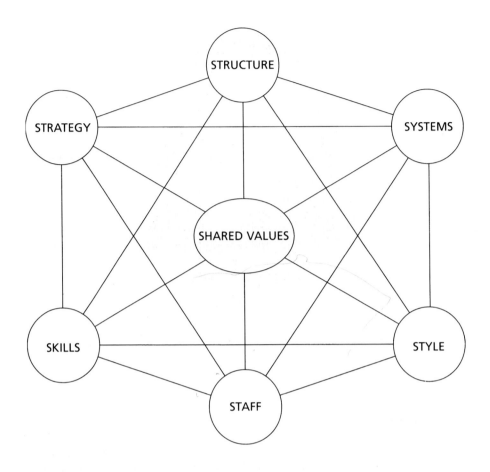

McKinsey's model of the role and tasks of the manager

imaginative construct. It could only be proven by scientific experiment if it were possible to reproduce in the laboratory the whole of the history of the planet and the development of organic life.

When Darwin first published this theory he was held up to ridicule by almost all his colleagues in the field, most of the general public and every religious activist. However, as time passed the number of individuals arguing against his theory became fewer and fewer. People have become intellectually accustomed to Darwin's construct and where it once seemed alien, it now makes perfect sense except to a few fundamentalists.

Research methodologies

Research methodologies can take various forms, as outlined below.

Charles Darwin (1809–1882)

OBSERVATIONS

This method records what happens in the real world and discovers how actions are perceived by those involved. The two main types of observation are:

- the open, or overt, method: those observed are aware of the observation
- the participant observer method: in this case the researcher becomes a member of the group and takes part in its activities, often without the other participants knowing the primary reason for this individual's presence.

SOCIAL SURVEYS

A survey is usually a verbal questionnaire or form of interview used to obtain information from large numbers of people. It is often undertaken in the street, and is particularly associated with consumables.

QUESTIONNAIRES

These are written lists of questions pertaining to the research either directly or indirectly and are taken from a large number of selected people.

INTERVIEWS

These may be:
- formal structured interviews: either questionnaires read out by an interviewer with boxes to tick with the appropriate choice from five or six answers, or a series of pre-arranged questions which can be answered in an open unpredicted way
- informal interviews: characterised by open questions. Interviewers may even follow up answers with further relevant enquiries.

DIARIES

Respondents are asked to keep a daily journal of events and feelings, over a particular length of time.

LIFE HISTORY

This could be a complete biography of someone or it could be aimed at major events in the person's life.

TIME-BUDGETING

This is used to discover how people structure their day and what they do at certain times, e.g. to determine how shift work affects people's lives. This is best done over a relatively short period of time as it can be time consuming for the respondents.

CASE STUDY

This is usually an in-depth study of a person or situation using interview techniques and some observations, for example Levinson's work described in Chapter 6.

COMMUNITY STUDY

This could be a study of a particular area or group. It could involve participant observation, interviewing and literature search methods.

EXPERIMENTS

Experiments are used to try and find out if one event causes another. The researcher has to try to examine one variable while keeping other factors the same. Experiments are of two types:
- *laboratory experiments*, which involve investigations where experimenters try and look at one particular aspect of behaviour under controlled conditions

- *field experiments*, which are experiments that take place in the real world. Those taking part may not be aware of the fact. Rosenthal and Jacobson's (1968) experiment to see the effect of teachers' expectations on pupils' performances found that if teachers thought pupils would do well, they treated the pupils differently and their subsequent performance improved.

Organisational behaviour

Organisational theory is used to explain how organisations work. The term 'organisational theory' has been widely used in the past 100 years, but the activity itself dates back to the Ancients – the Greeks and Chinese (from whom we have inherited many useful insights). Sometimes the term 'industrial psychology' is used to describe this activity, although this term also has more restrictive uses.

Generally speaking, organisational behaviour theories come from three perspectives:
- the organisational structure and functions
- the systems and procedures designed to cope with transactions and interactions in the organisation, and
- the individuals who work there.

The whole study of management is fraught with complexity. Theorists in this area are simply unable to competently control the many variables that confront them – no two people, no two situations are alike, nor can they be easily reproduced to test and re-test the findings.

Much of the evidence offered by management theorists is based on:
- *observations*, like those of Charles Darwin or the Hawthorne experiment (see Chapter 5)
- *experiments*, like those of Rosenthal and Jacobson (1968)
- *retrospective case studies*, like those of Holmes and Rahe (1967) and Levinson (1978)
- *one person's notion or good idea*, like Jack Stack's ideas about 'open book management'
- *models or paradigms,* which when shared with others have a certain common-sense appeal, like Maslow (1954) or Peters (1982).

These last two types of theory are easy to argue against or to prove invalid simply because they have not been adequately tested. However, if used with an open mind, such constructs are very useful as long as their status is well understood.

Structure, function and cultures in the work place

STRUCTURE

The term 'structure' refers to the way an organisation is formally put together – the official picture: who is the boss and who reports to whom.

The structure of an organisation depends on two important things:
- purpose, i.e. goals and objectives – what the company does/makes/sells/ services
- size.

It also depends on a series of much less significant things such as the history, the ownership, the staff, the economic climate, environmental factors and so forth.

Structure is usually presented diagrammatically for marketing purposes in literature published by many quite small organisations and by all large ones. This perception of the organisation may not be exactly as a management theorist would describe it.

The diagram below shows a simplistic outline of how most managers would represent the nursery structure – as a hierarchy or pyramid structure, one layer being supervised by the next smaller layer until a pinnacle is reached.

Purpose, goals and objectives

'Purpose' in childcare terms can be illustrated by the difference between managing a centre where the children are well, happy and busy with their development and managing a centre which involves caring for sick children or children at risk.

Management techniques in these two different centres will be differently focused, emergency procedures differently arranged, reporting systems slacker or tighter – the aim in one being to educate and care for the children, and in the other being to protect them and facilitate medical or social intervention. *A happy, relaxed and informal structure will prevail in one and a calm, carefully controlled, formalised and monitoring structure in the other.*

When studying general management theory you will often find the contrasts drawn between managing a hospital and managing a lawyer's office – that is, between a large complex bureaucratic structure and a 'look out for yourself' structure.

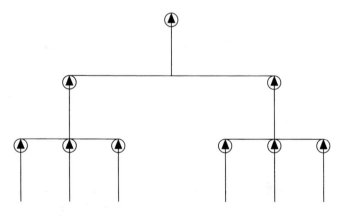

A typical hierarchy model used by a manager

Size

Size is the single most important factor affecting both the structure of an organisation and its cultures. Most childcare centres are very small in management terms.

Nonetheless, managing a 60-place children's centre operated by the local authority will be very different from managing a 20-place unit for a corporate nursery or a 30-place owner-run nursery or again managing a work-based nursery.

TYPES OF STRUCTURE AND CULTURE

'Structure theorists', including Max Weber (1921) who first described bureaucracy, and Roger Harrison (1972), together with the British theorist, Charles Handy (1986), detail four main structures and attendant cultures. They are generally called bureaucracy, autocracy, matrix and cluster structures.

(Note: In modern usage, the word 'bureaucracy' is seen as a negative term; here, however, it is used as a neutral term. Many workers enjoy the bureaucratic structure, which has, indeed, a great many advantages.)

The structure of each organisation is often associated with a certain culture or way of behaving:

- a bureaucratic structure is generally associated with a role culture
- an autocratic structure is generally associated with a power culture
- a matrix structure is generally associated with a task-based culture
- a cluster structure is generally associated with a person culture

Childcare centres which well illustrate each one of these structures and cultures can be found without too much effort.

Bureaucratic structure:

(*Role culture:* each worker knowing their individual role)

- local authorities including nurseries (social and educational)
- some of the large corporate nurseries
- sometimes work-based nurseries.

Autocratic structure:

(*Power culture:* being dominated by an individual who holds all the power)

- owner-managed nurseries
- small private schools
- some playgroups.

Matrix structure:

(*Task culture:* being focused on the task)

- some work-based nurseries
- some playgroups
- community nurseries.

(Community-run nurseries often work like this, as do parent/toddler groups. Someone is technically the boss, but everyone has an apparently equal say and there is no real power base or the power base is shared.)

Cluster structure:
(*Person culture:* where the person offers professional services)
- some emergency nanny agencies
- self-employed childminders
- some individual units within corporate nursery groups.

(Everyone is doing their own thing, running their own show but collecting work and support centrally from each other and using services that are collectively funded.)

ORGANISATIONAL CULTURE

The notion of organisational culture or ways of behaving was first described by Roger Harrison; he used the word 'ideology' but 'culture' is now in more common use. We retain the names he gave to describe each type of culture. He identified four:
- role ideology or culture
- power ideology or culture
- task ideology or culture
- person ideology or culture.

In any organisation (and that includes nurseries) groups of individuals over time develop ways of doing things – deep set beliefs about what is and what is not an acceptable way of working. These beliefs or norms of behaviour are what we are referring to here as 'culture' and they are a reflection of the same concept used in describing societies.

The culture of the organisation will affect what people are called (first or second names), how they are dressed (formal or informal dress code), how they work with the children and how they relate to the parents, the registration officer and any other person associated with the nursery.

Like structure, the culture of an organisation is dependent on both purpose and on size.

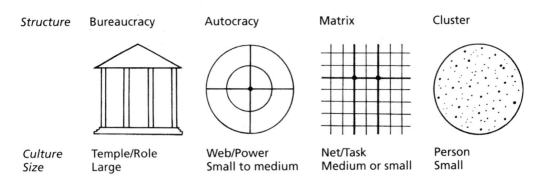

Structure	Bureaucracy	Autocracy	Matrix	Cluster
Culture	Temple/Role	Web/Power	Net/Task	Person
Size	Large	Small to medium	Medium or small	Small

Types of structure and culture

CASE STUDY

New staff joining any organisational cultures are given, either formally or informally (depending on the structure), an induction into 'the Somewhere way'.

'As a new member of staff in a very famous nursery I foolishly made a surprised comment on the expert performance of two-year-olds with their knives and forks. I was rebuked by the remark "we like good table manners, it is the Somewhere way". A colleague took me aside and said "you'll hear a lot about the Somewhere way – it isn't written down you know, it has seeped into the brickwork, you just wait until you pick it up by osmosis". Later, one parent told me that her child was totally incapable of using a knife and fork at home – was in fact still spoon fed – certainly the parent did not expect such behaviour at two. The little girl did not take "the Somewhere way" home with her.'

In the situation described here, it would be very hard for a new manager to change anything. In any case, good table manners constitute desirable behaviour and this serves to illustrate that not all cultural traditions demand change. The other interesting lesson to be learned from this example is the wonder of a small child, who at two years old knows that behaviour acceptable in one culture can be quite different from the behaviour acceptable in another.

This phenomenon can also be observed by students who move within schools from one room to another and find that even within the same school structure, cultures differ from room to room from staff team to staff team.

CASE STUDY

'I recall as a very junior student nurse being scolded on my first appearance on a hospital ward by a dragon of a Sister who completed her precautionary rebuke by saying "and don't think we will tolerate any of your sloppy Ward 3 ways here". Ward 3, although part of the same bureaucracy was an orthopaedic ward full of young and vigorous motorcyclists who had various broken bones but were otherwise in rude good health.

Needless to say the culture in that unit was quite different from the rest of the hospital and particularly from the acute female surgical unit presided over by the dragon.'

As this example illustrates, culture, like structure, is also very much affected by the purpose of the organisation. The culture in a reception class evolved to support and settle very young children differs from the culture in a secondary class designed to encourage a systematic learning environment.

It is dangerous to think that one culture is better than another. There is no right or correct culture for any organisation or any nursery any more than one country's culture is more right than that of another country. An individual might enjoy and feel more comfortable in one rather than in another but no culture can be right or wrong in itself. Just as individuals might be more comfortable in England than in France and more comfortable in France than in Japan, so staff will have a culture that suits them best and where they function well. The reverse is also true. People often complain of this, saying 'my face didn't fit'. They found themselves in an alien culture and unless they were prepared to change their own ways they would not fit in.

In setting out the idea of structure and culture in a diagram like the one above ('Types of structure and culture'), the whole area can be made to look very simplistic. However, it can actually become very complicated, particularly when the *culture* of one part of the organisation is in conflict with the *structure* of another part of the organisation. This can easily happen, as the following case study illustrates.

CASE STUDY

One work-based nursery had great communication difficulties because the hospital it served had a bureaucratic structure whereas the nursery left to itself was autocratic. In instances like this communication becomes a major issue – one side failing to grasp the view or the needs of the other. They are genuinely coming from different cultures – neither right nor wrong, only different.

Conversely, another large bureaucracy, a university, containing many matrices at its edges in clusters of task-oriented academics, could happily support, accommodate and communicate with a nursery that functioned as a matrix on most days and as an autocracy in times of crisis.

Activity
This activity is designed to develop understanding of structures.
(a) List the factors in your centre that you think influence the structure.
(b) Working with a colleague, verbally expand on your list and then on your colleague's list.
(c) Is this its first structure?
(d) Which structure might come next?

BUREAUCRATIC STRUCTURE, ROLE CULTURE

Bureaucracy was first described by the philosopher/sociologist and great German economist Max Weber in 1921. He described it as 'the authority of the eternal yesterday'. A bureaucratic structure and its dependent role culture is characterised by the jobs or 'roles' staff occupy – not by them as personalities, or as individuals, or even by their academic qualifications. It will be led by a Chief Executive. Two or more Deputies will be answerable to the Chief Executive and this group makes up the pinnacle of the temple shown in the diagram 'Types of structure and culture'. The pillars or poles supporting the pinnacle represent different departments/rooms or units/ centres. Each unit will have its own leader/head of department who, in turn, will have one or two deputies who will have staff answerable to them and so forth.

Advantages of a bureaucratic structure

Role culture and bureaucratic structure prevails in stable times. It is excellent for staff development and progression. It allows ambitious, talented, assertive individuals to climb steadily up the pillar, to have some sense of where they are going, and how well they are doing on the journey. They can be heard making such remarks as 'I was already a head of department by the time I was 30'. It is safe and in most instances people have jobs for life and pensions for retirement. It often provides sports facilities and other perks, increasingly private medical cover. It is paternalistic.

Disadvantages of a bureaucratic structure

Charles Handy (1986) notes that, like the Greek temple it resembles, the pillars of a bureaucratic structure will rock and crumble causing the whole edifice to tumble when the earth shakes. Bureaucracy needs stability to survive and hates change. It is argued that bureaucracy saps individuals' creativity and limits their horizons thereby causing alienation.

AUTOCRATIC STRUCTURE, POWER (OR CLUB) CULTURE

This is the traditional shape of a company started up and run by one individual. The leader holds the reins, has all the power and gives the name to the culture. Although it is generally shown as a web – the spider in the middle making all the silk and holding all the reins of the company – it adopts whatever shape the power-holder (the spider) feels happiest with. However much these structures vary, they have one common feature: they are dominated by one single personality (or sometimes one single family). They function by the power of personal loyalty. The quality in this culture is very much in the hands of the power-holder – good or bad. Staff can only join the club or leave.

This culture is the one most reported in newspapers when it gets to be any size and runs into difficulties, particularly because there is no control of the massive driving ego. These organisations are run by moguls who are confident of getting their own way and unless they are unfortunate they generally are successful in doing so.

It is important to notice that many large bureaucracies had their origins in the autocratic club culture of one energetic individual with a good idea.

Industrial historians take great delight in these famous names – Ford, Sainsbury, Cadbury, Coates, Fry, Dyson.

Advantages of an autocratic structure and power/club culture
This culture enables very speedy decisions to be made, minimises administration and is cheap to run. Money is spent where it matters. It values individuals and gives them their freedom. The reward for success is high.

Disadvantages of an autocratic structure and power/club culture
This culture is nepotistic, although this is not always a bad thing. It can feel very like a 'closed shop' if one is on the outside. It is paternalistic and fosters the 'cult of the individual'.

MATRIX STRUCTURE, TASK CULTURE

The matrix structure and its task culture is a relatively recent phenomenon. The strength of the matrix is at the intersections – where the networks cross. The structure draws resources from various parts of the organisation to focus on the knotty problems the organisation as a whole is constantly solving. The task culture is only interested in expertise that is applied by teams with specific responsibility within overall management strategy.

This structure is common among teams of interdependent professionals, e.g. academics; architects and surveyors; film makers, make-up artists and camera staff. In this context it serves to strengthen and facilitate the work of the teams.

Corporate nurseries sometimes demonstrate this structure. Frequently a 'set up team' exists working within an organisation waiting to move to a new site, using the specialist setting-up expertise and skills of purchasing, liaising with local authorities, supervising plumbers, builders and electricians and, indeed, the EYCDP Development Officer.

A 'take-over' team usually exists if the corporate nursery is currently in business. The purchasing corporate business will send in a team, who come in, take over the prevailing culture and then, when ready, will negotiate the change in culture to their own.

Advantages of the matrix structure and task culture
This structure is good for people who know their job well, who are enthusiastic and committed to teams. There is no place for private agendas. It fosters mutual respect and flourishes in times of change if, and only if, the economic climate is sound.

Disadvantages of the matrix structure and task culture
This structure is very expensive to run and has difficulty in developing systems and routines. It also tends to be short-lived and is slow to make decisions because all these taskmasters need to come to an agreement.

CLUSTER STRUCTURE, PERSON CULTURE

This structure is usually associated with professional legal or medical practices where workers may occupy the same space but do not strictly speaking form 'teams' as each individual operates for and by himself or herself. The structure exists only to host its members.

This is the only structure in which the individual is greater than the organisation. Hairdressers/beauticians are good examples. Emergency nanny services and groups of childminders are examples of this structure, as are consultants used in this sector to provide training, assessing and so forth.

Advantages of the cluster structure and person culture
This structure works well when success depends on the skill, talent and energy of members. It allows for personal identity to flourish. It allows for great flexibility and freedom and is considered to be a low-stress structure.

Disadvantages of cluster structure and person culture
In this structure there is very poor status given to some members of support staff, e.g. the practice manager, administrative staff. No manager has power to reward and this means that members are difficult to control and there is only management by consent. If members are not satisfied they will not hang on for the sake of the organisation – they are more important than the organisation and they will simply move on. If enough of them move on, the organisation will fold.

Activity
Work in pairs or groups of three.
(a) Make a structural and cultural diagram of your own organisation or centre.
(b) Label it appropriately.

KEYS TO GOOD PRACTICE
- Check that the structure of the nursery is in accord with the culture.
- Check that the culture of the nursery is appropriate to its function.
- Ensure that new members of the nursery are not excluded or made to feel they do not belong.
- Appoint a mentor to support new colleagues.
- Arrange a 'friend' for new parents and children.

5 THEORETICAL STRATEGIES APPLIED TO EARLY YEARS PROVISION

> **What this chapter covers:**
> - motivation theories
> - traditional theories of motivation
> - classical research studies
> - non-traditional theories of motivation
> - leadership theories.

This chapter is about the main academic organisational theories that underpin the management techniques in respect of the manager as:
- motivator
- leader
- support
- empowerer and, inevitably,
- controller.

As has been noted earlier, the pure research in management comes mostly from industry and spans the past century or so since the first management research was undertaken.

Knowledge of the theories of motivation is particularly pertinent in early years provision because of the need to motivate not only children and parents, and students and volunteers, but also the staff teams charged with delivering quality care.

Knowledge of leadership theory is pivotal to the manager's task in the nursery for it is on the manager's performance that the nursery's future and profitability depends.

Motivation theories

By 'motivation' we mean that which makes us *do* something – in this case, what makes us want to work, and, more specifically what makes us want to work *harder*.

The historical/theoretical perspective on motivation makes certain assumptions about a human being.
- He/she is a rational economic being, i.e. human beings are motivated by their own needs and are self-serving.
- He/she is a social being, i.e. human beings will be happier functioning within a group or team – we are gregarious/pack animals.

- He/she is a self-conscious being, i.e. human beings are self-motivating or self-starting and will make voluntary psychological contracts with the organisation.
- He/she is a complex, curious being and can respond to a variety of management strategies in unpredictable ways.
- He/she is a psychological being – human beings have evolved with the notion of the *ideal ego state*. We all hold in our heads a model of ourselves, an 'ideal ego', which will drive us to strive towards our image of the perfect self, well after basic needs such as hunger have been met.

If work is part of the identity of the perfect self – the ideal ego – then work will be undertaken constantly. This phenomenon is part of a theory sometimes referred to by sociologists as 'the Protestant Work Ethic' and in more common cultural terms as 'workaholism'.

'E' FACTORS

Organisational theorists have undertaken a great deal of research in this area, and have developed a motivation formula based on the notion of 'E' factors.

The 'E' in motivation theories represents:

- Effort
- Enthusiasm
- Energy
- Excitement

- Expenditure
- Effectiveness
- Efficiency.

The job of the manager as motivator is to activate or liberate as many 'E' factors in their staff as possible. There are a great many ways of doing this apart from the 'carrot and stick' approach, although these methods still have their uses.

Activity

In a group, brainstorm the notion of 'E' factors – see how many more you can think up.

Think of a group of people you know – a staff team, for example. How many 'E' factors can you attribute to each member of the group?

PSYCHOLOGICAL CONTRACTS

Workers have a psychological contract with their employers or with their organisation or with their job. (We all have many such psychological contracts, e.g. with family, with children, with the darts club, with the operatic society, with the church – and these are symbolised by the people we simply cannot let down.)

Psychological contracts work well for staff motivation if:

- the psychological contract with the job is more satisfying than any other the staff member may be holding currently (it rarely competes well with a new house, a wedding or a new baby so allowances have to be made at times of major life events)
- the psychological contract is viewed identically by both staff and organisation; it can then be depended upon by both sides and becomes both predictable and useful.

There are several varieties of psychological contracts.

Coercive contracts

In a coercive contract the 'E' factors are called forth by punishment, or the fear of punishment (the 'stick').

Calculative contracts

In a calculative contract the 'E' factors are called forth by reward, usually more money such as a bonus ('the carrot').

Co-operative contracts

In a co-operative contract the 'E' factors are called forth by the needs of the leader, the task or the organisation. The contract holder must therefore identify closely with the needs of the organisation, so we have the phenomena of the 'company man' and the 'vocational calling'.

It is not possible to force a co-operative contract on paid staff, they must pick it up by themselves. It is like responsibility – it cannot be given, it has to be taken.

The following activity will help you to work out some of your own psychological contracts.

Activity

Think of two different groups to which you belong. Answer the following questions in respect of both of them.

- What do they expect from you? List as many expectations as you can.
- Rank order these expectations starting with 1 as top priority, in terms of their importance to:
  — the group
  — yourself.
- What do you expect from them? List as many expectations as you can.
- Rank order these expectations in terms of their importance to:
  — yourself
  — the group
- Does this tell you anything about the psychological contracts you have with these groups?
- How could these contracts be different?
- Who would change them?

(Adapted from Handy, 1986.)

Traditional theories of motivation

There are three main traditional theories of motivation and we will discuss these in detail below:

- satisfaction theory of motivation – where the workers' mere passive satisfaction equals their productivity
- incentive theory of motivation – where rewards are given that call forth 'E' factors and result in more productivity ('carrot')
- intrinsic theory of motivation – where the job is worthwhile in its own right (in the opinion of the subject) and this will call forth 'E' factors and more productivity.

SATISFACTION THEORY OF MOTIVATION

This theory states that merely satisfied workers do not produce more, but they stay longer, and have better mental-health records than those who are dissatisfied. This, in turn, leads to less absenteeism and a small staff turnover. (In childcare this is an extremely important characteristic.)

This theory relates to the person who turns in day after day to do a fairly mundane job and works up to the hours they are being paid (the 'timesaver'). However, we note that these workers perform better when they like their leader and are satisfied with their group or team of colleagues. Human beings are, after all, pack animals.

Where staff are generally satisfied, greater effort can be called forth and greater productivity will result if they want to help others in the team – 'don't want to let the side down'.

CASE STUDY

There are some negative aspects of satisfaction theory.

Sometimes it happens that lower production than is possible will satisfy the team and output can be held down by group pressure.

'I recall a nursery unit where the supervisor was either busy working in her office or constantly nagging and seemingly extremely unsupportive to her staff. Nevertheless they were rarely off sick and seemed to stay forever. The practice in the nursery was fair, good enough to keep it ticking over, but not brilliant. The place was clean but not exciting. The staff seemed sombre, they arrived and they went on the dot.'

It took a change of supervisor and some management input, but no money, to stimulate this team to transform this adequate provision into the vibrant place it became.

INCENTIVE THEORY OF MOTIVATION

This theory states that productivity (effort) is called forth by reward (money). This will work if:

■ the worker thinks the effort is worth the money
■ the effort can clearly be attributed to the individual worker
■ the worker wants the reward, i.e. needs the money
■ any new effort will not become a new minimum production level with no extra reward attached.

This theory of motivation is rare in work with children although private nannies involved in unsocial working hours and in dangerous or difficult locations are often rewarded in this way.

INTRINSIC THEORY OF MOTIVATION

The intrinsic theory of motivation claims that a worker's own needs are motivators when *these needs are unsatisfied*. So, if a worker needs to gain personal recognition by the supervisor, they will work diligently until such recognition is given. If the worker needs to be in control to hold power, they will work diligently until they get to be in charge or to hold power even if that takes a whole working life. The motivation comes from within the individual.

The intrinsic theory cannot be used if:

- technology or structure prevents it, e.g. the worker is trapped in a structure or technology with no power to change things
- the workers involved have no self-actualising needs (i.e. are not upwardly mobile)
- the worker prefers an autocratic leadership style. A worker's preferences may vary at different times; a young inexperienced worker may feel more secure when strong guidance is available or a worker who currently carries a lot of family responsibility may not feel able to shoulder even more at work and may be glad to take directions.

This theory works best where people are self-starters, e.g. in research and development and with entrepreneurial business people who are constantly inventing new opportunities and challenges.

This theory is much in evidence in small, privately owned nurseries where individual workers are self-motivating. It can also be found in specialist unconventional centres, e.g. special needs units or sick children's provision.

Research studies

There are several important studies associated with motivation that have a particular significance for the childcare service:
- the Hawthorne studies in 1926
- Maslow's hierarchy of needs (1954)

- Herzberg's two-factor theory of motivation (1966, 1968)
- the psychological theory of the 'locus of control' (Rotter, 1966).

THE HAWTHORNE STUDIES

In the late 1920s a group of young women who assembled telephone equipment were the subjects of a series of studies, known as the Hawthorne studies, undertaken to determine the effect on their output of working condition, length of the working day, number and length of rest pauses, and other factors of the 'non-human' environment. The women, especially chosen for the study, were placed in a special room under one supervisor and were carefully observed.

As the experimenters began to vary the conditions of work, they found that, with each major change, there was a substantial increase in production. Being good experimenters, they decided, when all the conditions to be varied had been tested, to return the girls to their original poorly lit workbenches for a long working day without rest pauses and other amenities. To the astonishment of the researchers output rose again, to a level higher than it had been even under the best of the experimental conditions.

At this point, the researchers were forced to look for factors other then those that had been deliberately manipulated in the experiment. For one thing, it was quite evident that the young women had developed very high morale during the experiment and had become extremely motivated to work hard and well. The reasons for this high morale were found to be:
- the young women felt special because they had been singled out for a research role; the fact of this selection showed that management thought them to be important
- the young women developed good relationships with one another and with their supervisor because they had considerable freedom to develop their own pace of work and to divide the work among themselves in a manner most comfortable for them
- the social contact and easy relations among the young women made the work generally more pleasant.

A new kind of hypothesis was formulated out of this preliminary research. The hypothesis was that motivation to work, productivity and quality of work are all related to the nature of the social relations among the workers and between the workers and their boss.

The Hawthorne studies are seminal in that not only did the experiment tell us a great deal about why people work harder but it also gave rise to an analytic tool – the so-called 'Hawthorne effect' which asks that allowance be made in all observational studies where the subjects are aware they are being studied.

It is because of this work that much observational research work takes place through a two-way mirror or is undertaken by participating disguised researchers.

The message from the Hawthorne studies is clear: staff need to be affirmed as people who are valuable to the organisation. They need to know that an interest is taken in their work and they need praise for a job well done.

Cautionary note: It is not advisable to reward poor work, but it seems that any interest is better than no interest. (A comparison with attention-seeking behaviour in children springs to mind.)

The discovery that staff work harder if someone takes an interest in their work is extremely useful for any manager in a childcare setting.

CASE STUDY

A manager I knew told me:

'Based on the knowledge of Hawthorne, I have often set up regular meetings with staff in order for them to share their progress and to allow discussion of their work. This helps in various non-routine situations:

- if I am having difficulties adjusting to their style of working
- if we are together setting up a new venture, in this case the meetings are very frequent – probably daily
- the more difficult time they are having, the more frequent the meetings.'

The downside of this strategy is that it is difficult for staff to abandon the routine when the work is complete or the crisis over.

MASLOW'S HIERARCHY OF NEEDS

Maslow developed a motivation theory based on a hierarchy of needs. These can be represented as a pyramid with seven levels of need. Now read through the diagram on page 54 showing these.

According to Maslow, the most basic of these needs are the physiological – hunger, thirst, sex and so forth. The next level indicates needs that are more sophisticated than this – safety, belonging and so on. The third level is more refined still and so on until one reaches the pinnacle of needs, which he terms 'self-actualisation'.

Maslow's work is regarded as basic to motivational analysis and is often quoted because it models a great deal about human beings in all aspects of their lives.

There are, of course, critics of the Maslow model. We can all think of exceptions: the starving artist who finds the inspiration to paint and self-actualise despite hunger, the footballer who plays on and scores a goal only to discover later an injury – even a broken bone. But the fact that such exceptions are news says a lot about the general rule.

Higher level needs are a later evolutionary development in the history of the species. You will have noticed that the higher up the pyramid one goes

Maslow's hierarchy of needs (based on Maslow, 1954)

the more needs are linked to life experience and less to biology and the more difficult they are to achieve.

'Self-actualisation' seems to be a fairly modern concept; the more sophisticated we become the more we expect personal fulfilment.

It is important to consider Maslow's model in association with the notion discussed earlier of the psychological being, and to recognise that what actualises one person may not actualise another and that we are all complex beings.

One woman, for example, may be fully actualised by motherhood and may only use her work to add to that actualisation, by earning additional funds for child rearing, while another might need work outside her mothering task to affirm her own personhood.

> **Activity**
> Reflect on your own life or the life of someone you know intimately and try to identify a time when you or they were prevented from progression by psychological needs.

HERTZBERG'S TWO-FACTOR THEORY OF MOTIVATION

In the 1960s, the American theorist Hertzberg developed an idea to explain what motivates workers and, although it incorporated existing theories, it has attracted a good deal of attention. Herzberg is a very charismatic figure. He called his theory the 'two-factor theory of motivation'. His research was based on questionnaires and interviews.

Herzberg maintains that in any work situation, one can distinguish between the factors that maintain (dissatisfy) and those that motivate (satisfy) workers. The interesting thing is that these are not opposites of each other. Changing the dissatisfying factors does not turn them into satisfying or motivating factors.

Hertzberg divided into two groups the elements that the people he questioned claimed motivated them. He claims that one set answers the question 'Why work harder?' and the other set answers the question 'Why work here?'.

Set 1: Motivational factors	Set 2: Maintenance factors
(Satisfiers)	(Dissatisfiers)
Recognition	Salary
Achievement	Conditions
Responsibility	Policies
Advancement	Interpersonal relationships
Q Why work harder?	*Q Why work here?*

Where Set 2 conditions obtain, there is a low staff turnover and low rate of absenteeism, as in the case given for the satisfaction theory described earlier in this chapter

Where Set 1 conditions obtain, there is a great deal of activity, new targets, fresh appearance, new developments and much excitement as with the intrinsic theory described above.

PSYCHOLOGICAL THEORY OF THE LOCUS OF CONTROL

This theory, originally described by Rotter (1966), provides a further motivator: the need human beings have to be in control of their own lives (Rubin and McNeil, 1983).

For some individuals, events in their lives are seen as 'bad luck'. To become rich, you play the lottery. To get a good job, you need to know the right people. In other words, life events are attributable to external factors. This type of person is said to have an *external locus of control.*

Conversely, individuals with an *internal locus of control* attribute all events entirely to their own efforts or to their own shortcomings. They did not get the job because they gave a bad interview or there was a better candidate; they did not pass the exam because they did not study hard enough and so forth.

Those with an internal locus of control work harder and are more successful because everything is not left to luck, because luck does not play a significant part in their lives. One professional has noted that 'the harder I work, the luckier I get'.

It is useful for any manager to observe which staff have an internal and which have an external locus of control because the motivating techniques that can be applied in each case will vary.

Activity

Reflect on a team of people with whom you work closely. For each member of the team, ask yourself the following:

- Does he or she expect rewards from hard work?
- Does he or she expect rewards from luck factors?

Non-traditional theories of motivation

JOB ENHANCEMENT

Job enhancement (also known as 'job enrichment') is a technique used to make a job more interesting or rewarding to the worker, e.g. a nursery officer's job could be enriched or enhanced by adding responsibility for student supervision, for NVQ assessing, for curriculum planning or for health and safety. Support in any of these roles would also need to be offered. In terms of such support it is more feasible to offer training and allocate 45 minutes' regular supervision than to leave the staff member to try and undertake all these tasks alone. This strategy also has the desirable effect of extending staff experience.

GOOD PRACTICE

While the purpose of enhancement is to motivate the member of staff by making their job more interesting there is a spin-off benefit in that it is also a good method of delegating tasks and creating a forum for supervision.

QUALITY CIRCLES

A totally different approach to motivation is the idea of the *quality circle*, which was widely established in Japan before being adopted in America and Europe later.

The fundamental nature of a quality circle is to motivate individuals through participation in decision making and reinforcement of positive feedback of results. It is of most benefit to organisations where quality performance is largely a function of individual effort and attention. The quality control methodology (which is almost a ritualistic approach in Japan) requires considerable effort to establish and sustain.

A quality circle meeting

Quality circles are widely used in manufacturing industries. A quality circle comprises a group of people – both managers and workers – in a single area or department within an organisation, which meets regularly to study ways of improving quality and to monitor progress towards such goals.

It is a participative device and quality circles are generally established on a voluntary basis. Those volunteering typically make up about half of the direct and indirect workers involved in the activities of a particular department. They may be offered training in the analysis and identification of quality problems and problem-solving procedures. Once any training is completed, the circle is formed and is invited to tackle particular quality problems either nominated by the management or identified by the circle itself. Each quality circle will normally tackle a series of projects, one at a time, identifying quality problems and means of eliminating such problems and establishing targets to be achieved through quality improvement.

Wherever it is used, the quality circle approach rests upon the motivation of individuals and the organisation's efforts to improve quality through error reduction. The technique could easily be adopted by nursery managers because small staff teams already exist in most nurseries. The work of the quality circles would readily facilitate the quality control procedures outlined in Chapter 11.

OPEN BOOK MANAGEMENT

This motivating notion was developed in an engineering company in Springfield, Massachussets, USA in the early 1990s. The leader of that 800-strong organisation, Jack Stack, devised a management system that started when he ran a two-day seminar explaining the minutiae of the business to all the staff. He saw business 'like a small game' and claimed you could not enjoy the game unless you understood the rules. He wanted his people to enjoy the game so he explained the rules.

The company (or representatives of the whole company) meet every two weeks to see the open account books and so understand the game. At least they know the score because they know:

■ how much is coming in – money and orders
■ how much is going out – salaries and costs
■ what the bottom line is – the knowledge of a fall in profits bring out the 'E' factors, referred to earlier, without the need to resort to more complex methods.

Jack Stack states emphatically that the company has profit sharing and shared ownership but that it is not democracy. The leader makes the decisions. He claims that in terms of the history of staff motivation it is the obvious that everyone misses. The obvious is that when workers understand the rules they will play the game. It is dazzlingly simple if it works.

Activity
Consider the non-traditional theories of motivation:
■ job enhancement
■ quality circles
■ open book management.
Could any of these methods be applied to your nursery or centre?
Write notes on how you could implement these methods.

GOOD PRACTICE

Staff motivation is one of the most serious tasks of any manager.
Sometimes the best motivator is simply to roll up your sleeves and get stuck

in. This is particularly effective if a really unsavoury task is involved. In this way you are motivating by example.

Sometimes – sadly – you can only resort to apply Herzberg's famous third factor of motivation, which he calls K.I.T.A., standing for 'kick into action'.

To fully motivate staff, a manager should give them confidence in their jobs – by explaining the context of the work, giving confidence in themselves by praising work well done and giving challenges, and giving confidence in the team by treating everyone equally and by using the creativity of the team when tackling problems. Good motivators also show concern for staff in times of trouble and provide good examples by their own behaviour.

Leadership theories

What makes a good leader and how someone can learn to be a good leader are immensely important questions for any manager. Can you be a 'born leader'? Not surprisingly, there have been a number of attempts to quantify and qualify the characteristics of leadership.

CHARISMATIC LEADERS

Before we look at 'ordinary' leaders it is helpful to dispose of the notion of *charismatic* or magical leadership. Some individuals are said to possess a magical power that causes others to follow them. However, there have only been a few such people in the whole of our history and in the childcare context it is not enough to think in magical terms (except to exclude them).

> ### Activity
> In a group, brainstorm the names of people in history whom you consider to have had 'magical' powers of leadership – for good but also for evil.
>
> When you are clear about charismatic power, it will be obvious that most leaders are made and not born leaders – even if sometimes they already have some existing characteristics that help in their leadership.

THE TRAIT APPROACH

This represents the first major approach to theorising in this area, and its broad aim was to determine those personal attributes that make a person a leader.

A number of characteristics have been proposed as being advantageous (at least in men) including height, weight, an attractive appearance, self-confidence, and being well adjusted and intelligent.

However, several studies and reviews have demonstrated that the typical leader is only slightly more intelligent than the average member of the group. Most researchers discover that leaders are neither extremely authoritarian nor extremely egalitarian but somewhere in between. They are often taller (or very much shorter) than the group and do have an attractive appearance and self-confidence.

THE SITUATIONAL APPROACH

This approach emerged later and was an attempt to supplement and rectify some of the shortcomings of the traditional trait approach. For instance, the situational approach acknowledges that leadership involves leaders and followers in various role relationships and that there are several paths to becoming validated as a leader – 'Cometh the hour, cometh the man'. This approach has been superseded by later theories.

THE CONTINGENCY MODEL OF LEADER EFFECTIVENESS

In the 1960s there was a revival of interest in the personality characteristics of leaders, but this was a much more sophisticated approach than the trait approach and one which also represented an extension of the situational approach.

A major figure in this new approach was F. E. Fielder whose contingency model for the analysis of leadership effectiveness (1972) is mainly concerned with the fit or match between a leader's personal qualities or leadership style, on the one hand, and the requirements of the situation on the other.

Leadership style
Fielder saw style as either *task-orientated* or *relationship-orientated*.

He began by measuring the extent to which leaders distinguish between their most and least preferred co-worker (LPC) and developed a scale that gives an LPC score. This score determines whether a person is relationship-orientated or task-orientated.

- Someone with a high LPC score is relationship-orientated and still sees their least preferred co-worker in a relatively favourable light and also tends to be more accepting, permissive, considerate and person-orientated in relationships with group members (relationship-orientated).
- By contrast, someone with a low LPC/task orientated score sees their least preferred co-worker very differently, regards them unfavourably, and also tends to be directive, controlling and dominant in relationships with group members (task-orientated).

Best fit
Fielder then investigated the fit between these two styles of leadership and the needs of the situation.

The hypothesis that he tested is that the effectiveness of a leader is contingent or dependent upon the fit between:

- the leader's style – whether task-orientated or relationship-orientated as described in the LPC score

- the quality of leader–member relationships
- task structure
- the position-power of the leader in the organisation.

The *quality of leader–membership relationships* refers to the extent to which the leader has the confidence of the group and to the general psychological climate of the group.

Task structure refers to the complexity of the task and the number of possible solutions – the more unstructured the task, the more the leader must motivate and inspire members to find solutions themselves rather than relying on the back-up of their superiors or resorting to rules.

The leader's *position-power* refers to the power inherent in the role, e.g. the rewards and punishments at the leader's disposal and the organisational support for the leader from superiors.

From studies like this, theorists were able to conclude that when any individual is put into a position where a group of people has to depend on their efforts, they tend to accept the responsibility and the challenge – that is, they behave like leaders. Just as crucially, they are *recognised* as leaders by the rest of the group.

Compared with people occupying peripheral positions, leaders tend to:
- send more messages
- solve problems more quickly
- make fewer errors, and
- be more satisfied with their own and the group's efforts.

Fielder thinks leaders are made – not born.

Activity

Think of the most important leader you have ever worked with in your life and answer these questions:
- How did you know this person?
- How did he or she treat you?
- What did he or she do for you?
- What can you do to make yourself more like this person?

ADDITIONAL CHARACTERISTICS OF THE LEADER

Two additional personal characteristics have been added to trait theory in recent times.

One is that some leaders have the capacity to take an overview of a situation. The so-called 'helicopter view' means that they are aware of other factors that affect the work and are impinging on the situation. They *can* see the wood for the trees.

The second is the capacity to work with uncertainty, to, as Tom Peters puts it, 'roll with ambiguity' (Peters and Waterman, 1982). This is the ability to continue functioning well without a clear idea of what might happen and what the next step might be. This capacity allows for great flexibility and encourages a healthy response to change. This capacity in a leader has always been desirable but is now almost essential.

ADDITIONAL ROLES OF THE LEADER

The leader of a team, a small group, or a large organisation acts as an ambassador for the team or the group or the organisation. It is the leader's job to project the feelings and needs of members, to communicate their value and to demonstrate that the team he or she leads is the best, the most cohesive, the hardest working and so forth. The level to which the leader can fulfil this function will be used by those inside and out as a measure of the leader's worth and also of the team's worth.

This is one of the most significant tasks of any manager because, as a bottom line, we all want to be on the winning side and in the winning team.

GOOD PRACTICE

Role model: as a leader or manager, staff will inevitably copy or emulate you. This is a sobering concept but must be borne in mind constantly in the childcare setting because *as the staff are treated, so will they treat the children and from this modelling the children will be moulded.*

Although it is important to recognise that not everyone can fill every type of role, a helpful lesson from the theory for any nursery manager is that finding oneself in a position of leadership will actually bring out hidden talents. Certainly as far as research studies are concerned, it seems to be the person's position in the network and not their personality that accounts for their success in the leadership role.

CASE STUDY

'I once knew a nursery where the true leader was the cook. She allowed the manager to do the administration, she allowed the staff to look after the children but she controlled both and was consulted on all issues – she held the power. I have also worked in college where the true leader was the senior janitor – nothing happened without his approval.'

Activity
This activity is designed to develop your self-analysis skills.
Mark yourself out of ten for each word in the following list of terms often used to describe leaders and managers:
    EXTENSIVE EXPERIENCE
    ABILITY
    CASE STUDY
    DYNAMIC, CREATIVE APPROACH

DEDICATED AND HARD-WORKING
LOYAL
OUTSTANDING PLANNING AND ORGANISATIONAL ABILITY
STRATEGIC THINKING
ENTHUSIASTIC, WITH DRIVE
INITIATIVE
AMBITIOUS
FULL COMMITMENT AND PROFESSIONALISM
MATURITY
SELF-AWARENESS
ADAPTABILITY
HIGHLY MOTIVATED.

KEYS TO GOOD PRACTICE
- Ensure you always respect staff as human beings.
- Be sure to praise good work.
- Ensure you always treat staff justly and equally.
- Be ready to join in with unsavoury tasks, or to stay late and demonstrate by example your own commitment to the work.
- Avoid rewarding poor performance.
- Avoid victimising or favouring individual members of staff.
- Give staff individual time on a regular basis when they are undertaking difficult or new tasks, e.g.:
  - supervising special needs children
  - supervising and assessing students/candidates
  - supervising curriculum development
  - preparing for the Ofsted inspection
  - health and safety.

THEORETICAL STRATEGIES FOR MANAGING CHANGE AS APPLIED TO EARLY YEARS PROVISION

6

> **What this chapter covers:**
> - management of change in the childcare service
> - management of stress in staff
> - stress theories
> - management of stress in self
> - transitions as stressors.

This chapter is about the only sure thing in life, apart from death and taxes. It is about change. Just to survive, even in the most sanguine professions, change has to be lived with, even relished, as part of the dynamic nature of society. 'Change is the only constant.'

It is particularly difficult for front-line workers in childcare to cope with the changes in their own organisations and in the stressed lives of parents when the children they are caring for so desperately need stability and routine.

This chapter looks at the various facets of change and suggests ways of dealing with them. This will include stress, at an organisational level and staff level, and particularly at the manager's level.

Management of change in the childcare service

In recent years the childcare service, like all other services, has experienced an accelerated pace of change.

Charles Handy in his book *The Age of Unreason* (Handy, 1989) uses a frog metaphor: 'if you put a frog in water and slowly heat it, the frog will eventually let itself be boiled to death. We too, will not survive if we do not respond to the radical way in which the world is changing.'

It is part of the manager's role to identify those changes that will affect the work of the team and those that will not, or at least not yet. The manager should:
- identify changes that could affect the centre's work
- assess the urgency of such changes
- develop strategies to implement the changes
- resettle the team's procedures after the changes have been implemented.

Managers who are proactive (as opposed to reactive), will suffer less personal pain (stress) as a result of change.

Charles Handy tells us that 'to suffer fewer disturbances from the unexpected we must understand the past'.

In response to this atmosphere of change Tom Peters produced his text *Thriving on Chaos* (Peters, 1987) in which he extols us to enjoy and welcome change and to 'roll with the ambiguities'. Other organisational theorists suggest similar tactics, for the truth is we cannot control it – there is no choice but to accept it.

GOOD PRACTICE

The childcare worker must become two tactically different workers – (1) with the children: conserving routines, deploying systems and creating stability; and (2) with the organisation: introducing computers, accepting new forms of inspection, record keeping, training students, changing systems, changing their expenditure patterns and, in some cases, even changing their employers following take-overs.

Change in the childcare service therefore brings inherent role conflict and it is important for managers to be clear about this and not to make the mistake of thinking that the only way to sanity is to rush down the path of change. The children, their routines and the pattern of their lives, as far as the centre is concerned, should remain *stable* on a daily basis.

Transitions, in the best interests of the children, should be gradual.

Changes that could affect the service are:

■ changes in law, both children's and employment law
■ changes in the curriculum demanded by parents and Ofsted
■ changes in the health of the population locally or nationally
■ changes in training programmes for childcare workers
■ changes in economics affecting parents, salaries and funding systems.

On the occasion of any one of these events, the manager will be expected to lead the team to a new way of working.

A good example of multiple changes to the service was the 1989 Children Act. The implementation of this Act was particularly stressful, followed as it immediately was by other related changes, namely:

■ the nursery funding reform for four-year olds – the voucher scheme
■ school management reform – the option for schools to opt out of local authority management
■ training reform – the introduction of NVQs for childcare and education workers
■ curriculum reform – the introduction into schools of the National Curriculum and to nurseries of the Foundation Early Years Curriculum
■ standards reformed (or asserted) by the publication of the National Occupational Standards for Working With Young Children and their Families (the NVQ)

- acknowledgement of the economic recession and the effect on small businesses
- public awareness of HIV and body fluid procedures
- the ratification of the UN Convention on Children's Rights
- the appearance of the corporate nurseries
- incorporating EEC laws in the work place.

In London the situation was further complicated by the birth pangs of the newly identified education departments hastily set up following the demise of the ILEA in 1991.

The childcare world has been inundated with change from 1989 onwards, culminating in the introduction of the National Standards for Early Years in 2001.

Strategies to deal with such changes need to be developed.

A MNEMONIC FOR MANAGING CHANGE – CREAM

C Communication systems and consultation systems must work effectively in the organisation

R Responsibilities and duties of all staff must be understood by all personnel

E Effects must be monitored (using the evaluation system described in Chapter 11) and systems suggested in National Standards

A Aims and purposes of change – and the possible effects on the children – must be known and understood and considered seriously

M Morale must be maintained in the team (and consequently in the nursery.

As you can see, the ideas listed in the CREAM mnemonic are very much the strategies we have been examining so far and constitute good management practice, with a heavy emphasis on communication. The following section suggests some further strategies that will assist in developing non-threatening communications systems.

Activity

The aim of this activity is to learn to distinguish between rewarding and punishing behaviours.

Review the lists of behaviour given below and add any other punishing or rewarding behaviours that come to your mind. Think about your own inter-personal style and see how many of these specific behaviours you can identify in your day-to-day patterns of working with others. These behaviours also apply in your private life, of course, as well as in work situations. Then ask yourself the following, very blunt questions:

- To what extent do people voluntarily seek me out?
- To what extent do people take the initiative in contacting me, communicating with me, sharing ideas and viewpoints with me, including me in their personal and social activities?

The answers to these questions will give you the clearest possible indication of whether your management style is primarily that of a punisher or a rewarder. In the long term, a rewarding style of dealing with others tends to keep your own stress level to a minimum, it helps others to do the same; and it makes work life a pleasant, enjoyable, achievement-oriented process.

Rewarding behaviour

Talking positively and constructively
Affirming the feelings and needs of others
Treating others as equals whenever possible
Stating one's needs and desires honestly
Delaying automatic reactions; not flying off the handle easily
Levelling with others; sharing information and opinions openly and honestly
Confronting others constructively on difficult issues
Staying on the conversational topic until others have been heard
Stating agreement with others when possible
Questioning others openly and honestly; asking straightforward, non-loaded questions
Keeping the confidences of others
Giving one's word sparingly and keeping it
Joking constructively and in good humour
Expressing genuine interest in the other person
Giving others a chance to express their views or share information
Listening attentively; hearing other person out
Sharing one's self with others; smiling greeting others
Giving positive non-verbal messages of acceptance and respect for others
Praising and complimenting others sincerely

Punishing behaviour

Making others feel guilty
Soliciting approval from others excessively
Losing one's temper frequently or easily
Playing 'games' with people; manipulating or competing in subtle ways
Throwing 'gotchas' at others; embarrassing or belittling others
Telling lies; evading honest questions; refusing to level with others
Overusing 'should' language; pushing others with words
Displaying frustration frequently
Making aggressive demands of others
Diverting conversation capriciously; breaking others' train of thought
Disagreeing routinely
Restating others' ideas for them
Asking loaded accusing questions or
Overusing 'why' questions
Breaking confidences; failing to keep important promises
Flattering others insincerely
Joking at inappropriate times
Bragging; showing off; talking only about self

Expressing respect for the values and opinions of others	*Monopolising* the conversation
Giving suggestions constructively	*Interrupting*
Compromising; negotiating; helping others to succeed	*Showing* obvious disinterest
	Keeping a sour facial expression
	Withholding customary social cues such as greetings, nods, 'uh-huh' and the like
	Throwing verbal barbs
	Using non-verbal put-downs
	Insulting and otherwise verbally abusing others
	Speaking dogmatically; not respecting others' opinions
	Complaining or whining excessively
	Criticising excessively; fault finding
	Demanding one's own way
	Refusing to negotiate or compromise
	Ridiculing others
	Patronising and talking down to others
	Officiously supervising minor tasks

LOW-STRESS COMMUNICATION

Helping employees and colleagues to keep their stress levels down will help you to keep your own down. It will also help everyone to work more productively if low-stress communication techniques are adopted – and remember: an ounce of help is worth a pound of sympathy.

GOOD PRACTICE

A staff development session should be devoted to working harmoniously. Use the list of rules for low stress working which appear in the activity later in this chapter.

A good rule of thumb is to try to make as many of your transactions as you can relatively rewarding and positive for the other person. Of course, this is not always possible because of the nature of some kinds of problems, because some other people may lack the social skills necessary to co-operate in making transactions positive and because you occasionally need to take a strong position in opposition to others. However, over the course of your many transactions with your employees and your colleagues, you should be able to make the great majority of transactions go smoothly and comfortably.

This might seem such an obvious point as not to be worth mentioning if it were not for the fact that so many people who work together in organisations do not seem to grasp it at all. Many others can keep it in mind only under pleasant circumstances but lose their grip on it when the pressure is on.

Relatively few managers seem to have developed the skill of putting others at ease and helping them stay there through the course of a business transaction, especially one that presents difficulties for them personally.

Think of your own personal communicating style as being either punishing or rewarding for others according to their individual reactions to the ways in which you treat them. You can assess this quite simply by studying their behaviour towards you. In behavioural science terms a punishing experience is one an individual is not likely to repeat; a rewarding experience is one he or she is likely to want to have again. This means that, if the people with whom you are communicating usually experience their transactions with you as positive, affirming to their own self-esteem and productive for them personally, *they will usually come back for more*. If they do not like the results, *they will tend to interact with you as little as possible*. This principle provides a very simple way to assess your communicating skills and to make an inventory of the specific managerial behaviour that causes stress in others – as well as that which helps them reduce stress.

Management of stress in staff

The 'hindrance to change' list below reads like a straightforward list of the actual symptoms of stress. This is for the very good reason that stress for some is not only caused by change itself, but that individuals already suffering stress from other sources, e.g. life events, find change more threatening and distressing than others.

A MNEMONIC IDENTIFYING HINDRANCES TO CHANGE – COFFEE

C Conflict/cynicism
O Obfuscation
F Fatigue
F Frustration
E Envy
E Ennui (resistance through lack of interest).

It is the role of the manager to identify possible origins of stress in staff members and to prevent their condition affecting the working of the nursery and particularly the lives of the parents, who, in their turn, are also dealing with life events and other stressors.

STRESS AT WORK

Change is not the only source of stress at work. The following factors will also be influential.

1. Poorly defined jobs, tasks, responsibilities and ranges of authority in the nursery.
2. Prior history of conflict between two or more people or groups of people, e.g. staff of baby room versus those of toddler room.
3. Interdepartmental relationships that frequently place members at cross-purposes; traditional adversary relationships such as nursery staff versus teachers, administration versus social work.
4. Unreasonable levels of pressure and pace in the organisation – this refers back to change but is often a function of staff shortage.
5. Severe economic downturn that jeopardises the job security of organisation members.
6. Overly competitive climate fostered by top management and managers at various levels.
7. Favouritism shown by managers to one or two employees.
8. Punitive, accusatory or threatening style of treatment by a unit manager, leading to escapist behaviour such as blaming others and shifting responsibility – developing a climate of blame or blame outline.
9. Unclear or arbitrary standards for advancement and promotion in the organisation; inconsistent patterns of reward.
10. Lack of support in liaison with parents/carers or outside agencies.

> **Activity**
> Using the above list of ten items and this text as a resource find guidance on tackling each item. Work in twos if you find it helpful to discuss each area.

Stress theories

STRESS IN GENERAL

Stress has no single definition. However, Selye (1956) tells us it is the 'non-specific response of the body to any demand made on it'. This is commonly thought of as the physiological model of stress (see the diagram showing the body's stress responses).

Perceived stressor

Brain

↓

Hypothalamus

Pituitary

Parasympathetic
nervous system
(less active during
the stress reaction)

ACTH (hormone)

Sympathetic
nervous system
(motor signals
go immediately
to heart and other
organs,
muscles etc.)

↓

Bloodstream

↓

Adrenal glands

Adrenalin and related
hormones

↓

Bloodstream

↓ ↓ ↓ ↓ ↓ ↓

Stress hormones flow to all organs,
muscles and cells of the body

The stress responses mobilise the entire body for 'fight or flight'

In this school of thought, fathered by Hans Selye, it is maintained that in order to cope with the physiological aspects of stress one must know how the body reacts to stressful situations. Only by using this knowledge can the stress coping mechanisms be put in place (see the diagram of the two branches of the central nervous system).

The physiological effects of stress are:

- stored sugar and fats pour into the bloodstream to provide fuel for quick energy
- the breathing rate shoots up, providing more oxygen
- red blood cells flood the bloodstream, carrying more oxygen to the muscles of the limbs and to the brain
- the heart speeds up and blood pressure soars, ensuring sufficient blood supply to areas where it is needed

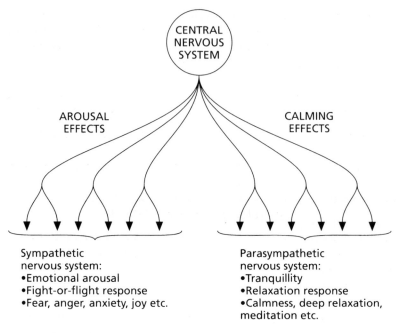

The two branches of the central nervous system work in opposition, alternately raising and lowering the body's excitation level (after Albrecht, 1979)

- blood-clotting mechanisms are activated to protect against injury
- muscles tense in preparation for strenuous action
- digestion ceases in order for that blood to be diverted to muscles and the brain
- perspiration and saliva increase
- triggered by the pituitary gland, the endocrine system steps up hormone production
- bowel and bladder muscles loosen
- adrenalin pours into the system.

These changes occur because of the basic nature of *Homo sapiens*. *Homo sapiens* is a psycho-physical being, i.e. the body and the mind are inextricably

linked. If the mind is stressed or put under any threat, like the threat of redundancy, the body will respond exactly as if it were being physically threatened. The 'fight-or-flight' mechanism which allowed our ancestors to survive as hunter-gatherers will come into play and the body will undergo the physiological changes needed to do battle.

Selye, who was the most influential stress theorist, described three stages of the General Adaptation Syndrome (GAS) – the body's reaction to stress.

Stage 1: Alarm   Integrated call-to-arms. Intense readiness and
                        mobilisation of biochemical resources
Stage 2: Resistance Vital resources applied to enable body to resist and
                        adapt to the stressor
Stage 3: Exhaustion Reversal to alarm stage in face of prolonged stress.
                        Results in wear and tear, or death.

The individual experiencing stress will respond in one of two ways by the GAS model of stress:

A enter stage 1 and progress to stage 2 and, assuming the individual copes with the stress, greater resistance will develop and growth occur, or

B enter stage 1 and, failing to cope by entering stage 2, move directly to stage 3 after which there is greater vulnerability and loss of resistance to stress in the future.

(See also the diagram showing the summary of stress interactions on page 75.)

Knowledge of the physiological model of stress does undoubtedly help individuals to understand more and to cope better when taken in association with the knowledge of human evolution.

COMMON CAUSES OF STRESS IN EVERYDAY LIFE

Holmes and Rahe (1967) devised a list of *life events* – a social adjustment scale compiled by interviewing individuals who had just experienced a life-threatening illness. The researchers' theory was that stress caused illness through a severe drop in the body's immune system. The drop was caused by the stress of a traumatic life event. They listed the events in the life of their subjects in order of seriousness and the effect they had on the subject. This work is a classic one and treated as seminal to any study on life stressors and although other researchers have adjusted the list the principle behind it remains unaltered.

Activity
Use the Holmes and Rahe life event inventory below to check out your own stressors over the past year.

It's worth giving serious thought to this exercise because it will help you to structure your life and work in the future.

SOCIAL READJUSTMENT SCALE

RANK	LIFE EVENT	MEAN VALUE
1	Death of spouse	100
2	Divorce	73
3	Marital separation	65
4	Jail term	63
5	Death of close family member	63
6	Personal injury or illness	53
7	Marriage	50
8	Fired at work	47
9	Marital reconciliation	45
10	Retirement	45
11	Change in health of family member	44
12	Pregnancy	40
13	Sex difficulties	39
14	Gain of new family member	39
15	Business readjustment	39
16	Change in financial state	38
17	Death of close friend	37
18	Change to different line of work	36
19	Change in number of arguments with spouse	35
20	Mortgage over $10,000*	31
21	Foreclosure of mortgage or loan	30
22	Change in responsibilities at work	29
23	Son or daughter leaving home	29
24	Trouble with in-laws	29
25	Outstanding personal achievement	28
26	Wife begins or stops work	26
27	Begin or end school	26
28	Change in living conditions	25
29	Revision of personal habits	24
30	Trouble with boss	23
31	Change in work hours or conditions	20
32	Change in residence	20
33	Change in schools	20
34	Change in recreation	19
35	Change in church activities	19
36	Change in social activities	18
37	Mortgage or loan less than $10,000*	17
38	Change in sleeping habits	16
39	Change in number of family get-togethers	15
40	Change in eating habits	15
41	Vacation	13
42	Christmas	12
43	Minor violations of the law	11

From Holmes and Rahe, 1967

*Note: figures published in 1967.

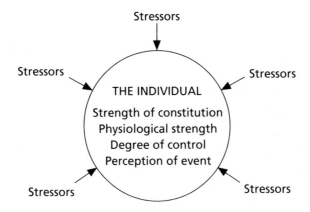

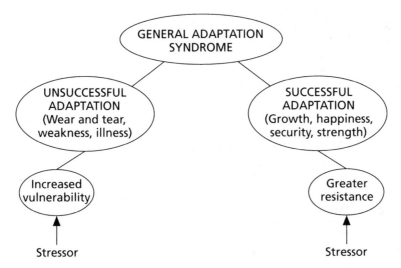

Summary of stress interactions

The Holmes and Rahe work can be very useful to the manager by helping with forward planning.

GOOD PRACTICE

If a member of staff is moving house, this is not the time to be putting extra work her way. It is not sensible to move house, change job and get divorced in the same week, and it is truly amazing how often this situation arises.

Some stressors will affect everyone. These are known as *normative stressors*. They include congestion, excessive noise, toxic fumes and other things that are well know to cause distress to all people.

Other stressors are unique to the sufferers or groups of sufferers and these are known as *ipsative stressors*. Stress resulting from the fear of heights, lifts, water or spiders comes into this category.

As the GAS model on page 73 illustrates, individuals who have successfully coped with stress will grow from the experience.

CASE STUDY

- The typical case cited of the man made redundant in his forties who takes the opportunity to start his own business and never looks back.
- The young nursing officer on the children's ward simply physically unable to cope with unsocial hours, demanding unhelpful husband and young children who retrained as a teacher, initially in order to accommodate the school holidays but who, as a result, enjoyed a long and successful second career.

The examples in the case study illustrate the adage 'from stress comes growth'.

However, the reverse is also true. One stress situation not accommodated leaves the subject weakened and less able to cope when the next trauma strikes.

In the case of work-related stress where the subject cannot cope over a long period, they will eventually succumb to the condition graphically described as 'burn out'. Burn out is a term used in both industry and social work to describe a state of apathy or ennui in which the subject becomes negative, detached and dysfunctional, both personally and professionally. It is very poor practice if a childcare worker demonstrating these behaviours is left in his or her post for this is both detrimental to the service and extremely harmful to young, or indeed any, children.

Management of stress in self

Activity
This activity is designed to enable you to develop rules for *low stress working* by focusing on work activities as a subset of life activities and developing a list of basic principles for working in a style that gets things accomplished with a minimum accumulation of stress points.

Use the list below as your starting point, adapt and add to it as you see fit and review it from time to time. Use it to review and assess the balance between what you give to your work and what you get out of it.

1. In the course of doing business, build rewarding, pleasant, co-operative relationships with as many of your colleagues and employees as you can.
2. Rate your work by order of importance and manage your time effectively; don't bite off more than you can chew.
3. Manage, by objectives, to capture the initiative on as many problem areas as you can.
4. Build an especially effective and supportive relationship with your boss. Understand his or her problems and help the boss to understand yours. Teach your boss to respect your priorities and your workload and to keep assignments reasonable.
5. Negotiate realistic deadlines on important projects with your boss. Be prepared to propose deadlines yourself, rather than having them imposed on you.
6. Study the future. Learn as much as you can about likely forthcoming events and get as much lead time as you can to anticipate them. Manage and plan proactively, not reactively.
7. Find time every day for detachment and relaxation. Close your door for five minutes each morning and afternoon, put up your feet, relax deeply and take your mind off the work. Use pleasant thoughts or images to refresh your mind.
8. Take a walk now and then to keep your body refreshed and alert. Find reasons to walk to other parts of your building or facility. Greet people you meet along the way.
9. Make a noise survey of your nursery area and find ways to reduce unnecessary racket. Help your employees to reduce the noise level wherever possible.
10. Get away from your nursery centre from time to time for a change of scene and a change of mind. Do not eat lunch there or hang around long after you should have gone home or gone out to enjoy other activities.

11. Reduce the amount of minutiae and trivia to which you give your attention. Sign only those things that really require your study, understanding and approval. Delegate routine paperwork to others whenever possible.
12. Limit interruptions. Try to schedule certain periods of 'interruptability' each day and conserve other periods for your own purposes. Make telephone calls and return all calls at a certain time (except for emergencies, of course).
13. Make sure you know how to delegate effectively. Make an inventory of a typical day's work and find out how many things you tended to do that could be assigned to someone else.
14. Do not put off dealing with distasteful problems such as counselling a problem employee or solving a human relations problem in your staff. Accept short-term stress instead of long-term anxiety and discomfort.
15. Make a constructive 'worry list'. Write down the problems that concern you and beside each one write down what you are going to do about it. Make a complete catalogue of current worries, so that none of them will be hovering around the edge of your consciousness. Get them out into the open where you can deal with them.

There are techniques that can be taught to allay stress. Courses are available and much work on the subject has been published. However, the level of success achieved using these depends on a knowledge of the physiology discussed earlier.

Relaxation as a stress management technique is taught on most courses and is widely available on tapes and videos.

Exercise and diet regimes that will help you feel better are often also recommended.

Assertiveness is also taught as a coping mechanism. The main strategy in coping with your own stress is to take charge of your own life – which is easy to say and can be hard to do. However, if you are physically fit, relaxed and assertive of your own needs, you are doing well.

Activity

This activity is designed to enable you to develop rules for *low stress living*. Study the list below and adapt it to produce your own list of rules for low stress living.
1. Make time your ally, not your master.
2. Associate mostly with gentle people who affirm your personhood.
3. Learn and practise the skill of deep relaxation.
4. Use an aerobic exercise such as jogging to build your health to a high level of conditioning.
5. Manage your life as a total enterprise, much as you would manage a corporation.
6. Do not become lopsided in any one area; seek rewarding experiences in all dimensions of living.

7. Engage in meaningful, satisfying work.
8. Do not let your work dominate your entire life.
9. Get your body weight down to a level you can be pleased with, and keep it there.
10. Form and keep sensible eating habits. Use sweets rarely, minimise your consumption of junk foods and eat more foods you like that are good for you.
11. If you smoke, stop completely.
12. Use alcohol only for social or ceremonial purposes, if at all; do not let it use you.
13. Eliminate the use of recreational drugs.
14. Free yourself from the chemical tyranny of tranquillisers, sleeping pills, headache pills and other central nervous system depressants.
15. Free yourself from dependency on patent medicines such as antacids, laxatives and cold remedies by teaching your body to relax and normalise its functions.
16. Have an annual physical examination to provide extra peace of mind.
17. Jealously guard your personal freedoms – the freedom to choose your friends, the freedom to live with and/or love whom you choose, the freedom to think and believe as you choose, the freedom to structure your time as you see fit, the freedom to set your own life's goals.
18. Find some time every day – even if only 10 minutes – for complete privacy, aloneness with your thoughts and freedom from the pressures of work. Preferably do this for a few minutes several times a day. Maintain 'stability zones', personal rituals and comfortable patterns that insulate you somewhat from future shock.
19. Do not drift along in troublesome and stressful situations. Rehabilitate a bad marriage or else end it. 'Fire' those friends from your life who are not really your friends. Take action to settle those matters that are troubling you. Do not leave troublesome situations unresolved for so long that they make you worry needlessly.
20. Have one or more pastimes that give you a chance to do something relaxing without needing to have something to show for it.
21. Open yourself up to new experiences. Try doing things you have never done before, sample foods you have never eaten, go to places you have never seen. Find self-renewing opportunities.
22. Read interesting books and articles to freshen your ideas and broaden your points of view. Listen to the ideas and opinions of others in order to learn from them. Avoid 'psychosclerosis' (also known as 'hardening of the categories'). Reduce or eliminate junk television watching.
23. Form at least one or two high-quality relationships with people you trust and can be yourself with.
24. Review your 'obligations' from time to time and make sure they will also bring rewards for you. Divest yourself of those that are not good for you.
25. Surround yourself with cues that affirm positive thoughts and positive approaches to life and that remind you to relax and unwind occasionally.

LEARNED HELPLESSNESS

Another classical theoretical research project that supports this work also gives insight into management stressors and suggests explanation of the executive illnesses: gastric ulcers, heart conditions etc.

This psychological study encompasses the notion that one will become 'helpless' when repeated situations occur in which one is powerless to act. A laboratory experiment was performed where two monkeys were harnessed together. Monkey 1 was able to respond to stimuli and, assuming he was adept, prevent both himself and Monkey 2 from receiving electric shocks. Monkey 2 could do nothing to help the situation and in a very short time he would accept anything that happened to him without resistance. He had learned to be helpless. In every other way the monkey was healthy and thriving, if not exactly full of initiative.

Monkey 1, the so-called 'executive' monkey, who was forced to take responsibility for protecting himself and his partner, was found on post-mortem to have severe gastric ulceration due to prolonged stress and anxiety. This experiment is often cited to explain the stress managers suffer as being due to the sheer complexity of their role – because they are taking it very seriously and because they feel the responsibility of their team and the need to provide for them.

The notion of learned helplessness is also used to explain the apathy of people in hostage situations and sometimes the depression of long-term, unrelenting unemployment. The findings in this area are also very relevant for workers involved with vulnerable people.

TIME MANAGEMENT

As mentioned earlier, you need to learn to make time your ally not your master. As stress is often associated with time pressure, time management is often a beneficial technique to learn in order to reduce stress. It is concerned with being properly focused and able to accomplish your highest priorities. Management planning is the single most important factor in saving time in the nursery.

Most of us have had the dreadful experience of being busy all day but getting very little accomplished. If this happens very often to you, you may feel as if you have no time to plan. However, you must conquer this belief because once you have mastered a few techniques and developed some discipline in applying them, you will discover that you cannot afford not to plan. The time you take to organise yourself will pay off with a more organised nursery, fewer forgotten tasks and a more relaxed approach.

Activity

Work through the following checklist, which looks at how you may be mismanaging your time. At the end of it work in pairs to:

- critically analyse your partner's response
- suggest techniques to combat your problems
- listen while your partner reciprocates.

Tick those boxes that apply to you

Putting things off	☐
Worry	☐
Lack of confidence	☐
Unscheduled meetings	☐
Guilt	☐
Idle talk	☐
Lack of direction	☐
Inadequate planning	☐
Time on the telephone	☐
Not listening	☐
No written goals	☐
Depending on written notes	☐
No using set forms	☐
Constant checking of staff	☐
Not setting deadlines	☐
Indecision	☐
Poorly run meetings	☐
Lack of delegation	☐
Fatigue	☐
Perfectionism	☐
Unclear goals	☐
Poor control	☐
Poor writing skills	☐
Doing others' work	☐
Not using 'prime time'	☐
Unclear communication	☐
Long lunches	☐
Not using time-saving devices	☐
No routine	☐
Cannot say 'no'	☐

Good time management can:
- simplify your life
- reduce stress
- increase efficiency
- improve job satisfaction
- improve quality of service in self and staff
- create more personal time.

Be aware of your own weaknesses in relation to time management.

The trick is to attack the problems you have as soon as you are aware of them.

■ Find out how you actually use your time (keep a diary for a set period).
■ Analyse the use of the time.
■ Sort your tasks and actions in terms of what is important to you and your job.
■ Identify tasks/actions that waste your time and eliminate them by delegation or negotiation.
■ Organise your time and energy to accomplish what is important to you and your job.

However, before you can begin to plan, you must realistically assess the constraints upon you.

■ Some things *must* be scheduled during fixed periods. Work with suppliers, parents and so forth will have to be completed during business hours.
■ Avoid planning anything for peak hours, such as dropping-off or picking-up times or children's lunch time.
■ Some management tasks require certain environmental conditions in order to be completed effectively. If you are trying to do work that

requires concentration, find a time and place where you will not be interrupted.

- Certain tasks will require the use of equipment or records that are only available at set hours and this will limit the time periods in which you can do this work.
- Understand your own rhythm and work patterns; as you become better at planning your time this will come more naturally.
- Nursery planning meetings with all staff will need to take place when the nursery is closed. Techniques to achieve this are explored in Chapter 8.

GOOD PRACTICE

Planning techniques will only work for you if you develop your own to suit your working style and actually use them.

- Establish a regular planning appointment with yourself. This could be a once-a-week session (e.g. the last thing on Friday or the first thing on Monday), or a shorter daily session, or a combination of these.
- Schedule similar tasks together. If you have a number of letters to write or a number of telephone calls to make, try doing them all during the same time period.
- Establish a regular 'quiet time'. Let other people know that you do not wish to be interrupted during specific times.
- Eliminate distractions from your field of vision. Place your chair so that you will not be distracted every time you see children and colleagues passing by – they can constantly distract you from the task at hand.
- Anticipate the things you will need (e.g. files, registration forms, copies of curriculum) and have them within reach before you begin work. Every time you break your concentration to find something else you need, you must spend time getting back into the rhythm of the work.

Do not insist on perfection in your planning. A system that has flaws will still be worth using. Work gradually with your faults. Effective time management can help you to simplify your life but only if you respect your own ways of doing things. The techniques you adopt should be adjusted to fit your own personal style otherwise they simply will not work.

Use the following ideas in order to keep paperwork under control.

- Do the work right after the task is given to you. Such instant action will fend off any tendency to procrastinate and let work pile up. You may have to refine your work later but, having started the task, you will find it easier to return to it promptly.
- Try to handle each piece of paper only once. Make a decision about the destination of each form, letter or circular the first time you see it. This is extremely hard to do but try, when you receive your mail and immediately you have understood the contents of it, to do one of the following things – *bin it – delegate it – file it* (a) for long term (b) for further action.
- Remove sources of frustration. If you have to spend time tracking

resources and gathering additional information before fulfilling an assignment, you are more likely to delay doing it. Gathering information makes the project seem more burdensome than it is. Try to get it in proportion: understand clearly all personnel and budgetary support available to you and where supplies and equipment can be found. Do not be afraid to request additional resources, supplies or guidance if you need them.

If the nursery is fortunate enough to have a secretary or an administrative assistant (or a share in one), you are way ahead in your struggle with time. A secretary can help not only by taking over certain tasks but also by helping you to maintain self-discipline and avoid panicking. Before a secretary can do this for you, however, you need to spend a certain amount of time together negotiating workable systems. Paradoxically, this is another burden on your time at first. However, investing time in training the secretary will pay off. If the secretary understands the nursery systems and why they are in place, then he or she will do things in a way that is consistent with how you would do them yourself.

CASE STUDY

'In our nursery, if follow-up action is needed for a task, we make a note of it in the nursery main diary. For example, if we expect a reply to a letter from a parent in, say two weeks, we write "Follow up with Janet" in the diary two weeks from today. If the follow-up will probably be by telephone then we have the number handy and write that down as well.'

Transitions as stressors

While it is neither desirable nor appropriate to be involved in the private life of staff members it is still advisable to be sensitive to how their life and career development is progressing and what effect their developmental stage may be having on their work and involvement with the organisation. In order to do this it is useful to understand the stages which individual staff members may be going through at any one time.

HUMAN GROWTH AND DEVELOPMENT IN ADULT LIFE

D. J. Levinson undertook a long-term study of adult development using retrospective case studies and a ten-year observation period. The results of this study were published in a book called *The Seasons of a Man's Life*. Levinson's study revealed that adults, like children, have *ages and stages*.

With the Levinson model, each stage has tasks that the developing adult undertakes. Some of these stages are characterised by change (transition) and some by stability.

The ages and stages that Levinson identifies are as follows:

Early Adult Transition (Adolescence), 17–22
Moving from pre-adulthood to early adulthood.
Developmental tasks
1. Move out of the world of childhood. Change childhood relationships with family. Leave behind childhood peer groups.
2. Move into adult world and explore, test out some choices, e.g. choose first career.

Early Adulthood Life Structure, 22–28
Entering the adult world.
Developmental tasks
1. To explore a new world, travel, work out alternatives, find adventure, e.g. seek places of entertainment.
2. To create a stable life structure, e.g. find a partner.

Age Thirty Transition, 28–33
Becoming a 'real' adult.
Developmental tasks
1. To reaffirm choices already made.
2. To make changes (remedy 'flawed' decisions), e.g. start new career, new partnership.

Second Adult Life Structure, 33–40
Settling down to fully fledged adult life.
Developmental tasks
1. To make a place in society – have a skilled job, develop a family life, e.g. have children, make a home.
2. To 'make it' in the world – strive to advance, to be affirmed by the tribe, e.g. get a more senior job.

Mid Life Transition (Mid Life Crisis), 40–45
May not affect everyone to the same extent.
Developmental tasks
1. To question achievements/choices: 'What have I done with my life?', 'What am I getting from my job, my family?' 'What do I want from life?'.
2. To find a new path through life, or to modify the existing path, e.g. may now find a new partner.

At the end of this stage changes will have occurred – maybe one big crisis or many small changes or adjustments.

Middle Adulthood, 45–50
Building a new life structure.
Developmental tasks
1. To be less dominated by ambition/passion.
2. To be more bonded to others.

Age Fifty Transition, 50–55
Developmental tasks
1. To review decisions made at 30 and adjust these if they are flawed.

Completing Middle Adulthood, 55–60
Developmental tasks
1. To rejuvenate oneself, enrich life, e.g. maybe new home or car.
2. To achieve some fulfilment, e.g. successful children.

Late Adult Transition, 60–65
A period of significant development.
Developmental tasks
1. To conclude the efforts of middle adulthood, e.g. wind down working life.
2. To prepare for the time still to come (retirement), e.g. find new skills for retirement.

It is important to note that whilst each period may be flawed because of developmental work from previous periods that has not been done, each new phase offers the opportunity to change, adjust, modify and to make a better life.

The identification of where you, and also your staff, are in your life and career development and assessment of how well you are progressing with your tasks will allow a pattern to emerge and will assist you in taking charge of your life.

KEYS TO GOOD PRACTICE
- Be aware of stress symptoms and intervene if any member of staff is unable to leave such symptoms outside the nursery.
- Be prepared to keep an open mind about the change process.
- Be clear that sudden change is not in the best interests of the children and be prepared to argue for time to change in a responsible way.
- Encourage staff development around the need to take charge of your own life.
- Be sensitive to major events in the lives of staff and adjust demands accordingly.
- Be sensitive to your own needs, guard your own time and pace your work.

PART III

7 SYSTEMS FOR ADMINISTRATION IN EARLY YEARS PROVISION

What this chapter covers:
- administrative systems for managing the children's records
- a system for nursery administration
- use of technology
- marketing the nursery
- strategic planning.

This chapter is about the sort of routine tasks that in themselves seem very boring but without which the nursery cannot function. The areas discussed in this chapter would come into the 'science' side of the great management divide between the 'science' and the 'art' of management.

It is vital to make administrative systems work in support of the early years services and not in opposition to them. The routines set up should improve the care given to the children and not be at its expense – either because the administrative work takes staff away from the children or because it becomes overly bureaucratic (in the negative sense of that word) and stress-inducing.

However, there is no getting away from the fact that the administration has to be done – the fees collected, the salaries processed, the rotas devised, the bills paid and so forth. The skills needed in this area must be acquired. It is a bit like the Highway Code – you might find it tedious to learn but you will not be able to drive unless you do.

Administrative systems for managing the children's records

Every early years centre needs systems for records that must be kept under the 1989 Children Act. Such records must be available for inspection by Ofsted at any time. These are changing, working documents and all staff should have access to and be familiar with them.

REGISTERING THE CHILDREN UNDER THE NATIONAL STANDARDS

A procedure for registering the children must be set up and records of the following kept. If you store these on disk a hard copy should also be available:

- full name, address and date of birth of each child attending or being looked after on the premises (hold in card index and child's individual file)
- names of the parents/carers, home and work telephone numbers (hold in card index and child's individual file); some centres also ask for photographs
- an emergency contact number and details of the emergency contact person (if different from above) and any other person authorised to collect the child (hold in card index and child's individual file); some centres also ask for photographs
- information about the religion, ethnic origin, culture and language(s) spoken, if the parent/carer is prepared to provide this (policy available, procedure recorded and on child's individual file)
- information about any health problems or other special requirements, e.g. diet, that the child may have (hold in card index and child's individual file). Display dietary requirements in kitchen
- name address and telephone number of family doctor and health visitor (hold in card index and child's individual file)
- consent form for outings and car journeys, to be held in child's individual file
- consent form for the administration of medication if appropriate (see Sample 27 on the CD-Rom), to be held in child's individual file
- a record of any medicine administered to the child, to be held in child's individual file.
- a record of allergies and treatment of same if condition requires.

In the nursery

It is both practical and sensible to devise standing forms for use in day-to-day affairs. Forms for parental permission should be devised using the samples provided as models. A standard package of permission/approval forms should be kept in a neat file and these discussed with parents when each child is admitted into the nursery. It is important that parents understand the implications of their signature.

See Samples 16, 21, 23, 24, 26, 27 and 28 on the CD-Rom.

Other records that should be kept are:
- a daily record of attendance and discharge (policy available and procedure recorded)
- a record of child protection concerns (policy available and procedure recorded)
- an accident/incident book (procedure recorded and in child's individual file)
- a record of the food served every day (policy available and procedure recorded). Menu displayed
- a record of fire drills and safety checks (procedure recorded)
- names and addresses of staff, assistants and key suppliers (on file)

- in the case of centres that are daycare providers, names and contact details of the board of directors and management committee or group (on file).

A system for nursery administration

In the administration of a nursery four simple basic systems are required, as detailed below. Of course, these may well be available on computer – however not everyone will have access to the machine and systems have been known to crash. It is therefore important to have records also available in paper form.

1. A card index system:
   - for the children's details
   - for general details such as suppliers and emergency services.
2. A filing system:
   - for children's records
   - for staff records
   - for the premises
   - for budgets/accounts and financial planning
   - for forward planning.
3. A display system
   This is necessary because much of the work must be displayed to meet the needs and in the spirit of the 1989 Children Act, the National Standards and the Ofsted systems.
4. A book system
   Various books are also needed:
   - minor accident book
   - accident and emergency book
   - duty rota book
   - log book (for recording day-to-day events)
   - petty cash book
   - incident book
   - fire drill book.

CARD INDEX SYSTEM

Children's details
This box should be stored by the telephone and should contain a card for each child with the contacts to be used in the event of illness or other emergency.

General
This box should also be stored by the telephone and should contain emergency numbers for plumbers, electricians, non-999 police, staff home numbers, i.e. numbers for any emergencies not connected to individual children.

It is perfectly possible to keep these indexes in the same box if space allows and there is no issue of confidentiality, e.g. in the case of sharing an office with another facility.

Card index systems are only useful if they are kept up to date and all details are recorded on the cards themselves and not on messy notes or post-it stickers. The responsibility for the card index should be structured into the manager's workload or delegated to a member of staff who will check it routinely.

FILING SYSTEM

Children's records

Records for each individual child must be kept under the 1989 Children Act and for the Ofsted inspection. These should include:

- a developmental progress record (see Sample 34) for the child to proceed with to his or her school
- a health record, and
- a social record – likes/dislikes and so on.

Staff records

Individual files should hold:

- the application form
- references
- photocopies of all vocational qualifications signed to indicate organisation has seen the original
- record of sending police check (the actual police check form is retained by, and is the property of, the authority)
- copies of qualifications and CV
- salary details and increments
- record of hours worked if member of staff is part time (see Sample 41)
- holiday and absentee records (can be held in this file or in a card index, depending on the size and complexity of the organisation)
- copies of appraisal forms, or records of when appraisals happened if the policy is not to record appraisals
- records of any courses taken as in-service training or at the expense of the employer
- records of any written warnings that may have been issued.

The general staffing file will hold:

- advertising for staff – records of previous advertisements, advertisement artwork and so forth
- sample job descriptions/person specifications
- blank police check forms
- health check forms
- staff development file, including details of courses offered locally by Early Years Development and Childcare Partnership and nationally.

BUDGETS/ACCOUNTS AND FINANCIAL PLANNING

For small nurseries a simple double-entry book-keeping system will suffice for records of income and expenditure (see Sample 22). The important thing is to monitor the cash flow, invoice the parents on time (see Sample 25 on CD-Rom) and keep a careful check that they pay within the specified period. Encourage a culture of prompt settlement of accounts. Sample 21 on the CD-Rom outlines financial procedures and can be adapted to fit your own situation. Set up standing orders if possible. Most parents will happily comply with that.

Records of income can be used to work out anticipated income from occupancy rate prediction. Occupancy rate prediction is undertaken by a forward-booking system and can be accurate for one month or one term only (or whatever period is paid for in advance). An occupancy chart should be completed to predict the income and highlight the vacancies.

There are excellent software programmes to undertake this task but a good understanding of the process is needed.

Activity

This activity is designed to develop skills in budgeting.
(a) Construct a sample budget based on a nursery or daycare centre you know.
(b) Examine the budget critically.
(c) Suggest any improvements.

Using a planning programme allows income prediction. It also demonstrates that full-time children make income prediction simple. So, from a business point of view also, full-time children make more sense. However, any empty place is undesirable because it indicates a lost earning opportunity. Vacancies can be compensated for if savings are made on staff, e.g. if the nursery is not busy on one particular day it may be possible to use that time as off-duty for staff or to balance the use of part-time colleagues. Although staffing represent the greatest cost to the nursery business, the same heating and lighting costs are incurred whether or not the nursery is full. The same equipment is still available, even when it is being underused.

For example, an applicant wants a space for an under-two child on Monday, when six children are already booked in. If you accept the booking for Monday this means an additional member of staff must be employed on that day. It is therefore in your interest to suggest Tuesday instead, as eight children are booked for Tuesday and three staff must be employed anyway as the number of children already exceeds six.

COSTING THE SERVICES

It is important when costing services that you remember the fact that parents will not wish to pay for holidays, whether bank holidays or summer

holidays. However, you will still have to pay the staff, the rates and all the other expenses for these holidays. In calculating fees make sure you take this into account.

Therefore if your fees (to cover all costs and meet all the nursery objectives) are to be £20.00 per day, the following equation should be used:

$$\text{£20.00 per day} \times 365 = \frac{7,300}{343} = \text{£21.28}$$

By dividing by 343, you are compensating for 8 days' bank holidays and for 14 days' annual holiday. Therefore, the true price per day you would charge is £21.50. Since the mornings tend to be more popular with parents the suggestion is that the morning charge is £11.50 and the afternoon £10.00, although this will vary with local conditions and many other factors.

FORWARD PLANNING

Plan occupancy as far ahead as possible – at least three months in advance. You can use computer programmes or a standard pro-forma to manage the waiting list. Suggest attendance alternatives to parents where it will help to balance the occupancy.

A sound system for forward bookings is vital whether it is kept in hard copy or on disk.

GOOD PRACTICE

Time must be set aside each week to analyse the loading on the nursery balanced against the staffing and other costs. Steps should be taken to reduce staffing levels if the fees do not justify the expenditure, e.g. by employing part-time staff or by reducing the hours of the full-time staff if possible.

A system that you are comfortable with should be devised to facilitate forward planning and to estimate loading on spaces.

MANAGING THE WAITING LIST

When nursery managers claim proudly 'we have a long, long waiting list' the statement should be heard with an appreciation of the following. In some cases the waiting list comprises children not yet old enough to attend, so they are not actually 'waiting' for a place today, but for a place in September when a whole group of children will be progressing to school. So the centre is not actually over-subscribed.

Many parents are perfectly happy to reserve a place for their child in every available nursery in the area so that they keep their options open. So the 'waiting' child may never actually appear in September. It is a good idea when a family is reserving a place for a child to ask for a substantial deposit – to be deducted from future fees but not returnable. This will give confidence to real applicants that a place will be there for their child when the time comes. They have paid for it after all. It will also deter some (but not all) parents from multi-booking. It will also give you some financial compensation for cancellation and buy time to find a replacement if indeed you are able to keep a 'real' waiting list.

As we have noted elsewhere, full-time children are the most desirable booking to have for many reasons. Many parents are aware of this and initially will ask for a full-time place and pay in advance for this, intending that the child should become part time in the next fee period. The child may never attend full time. There are many reasons for this – the parents don't work full time, the child spends some time with other carers, and so forth. This means that the nursery in the second fee period will have vacancies and will depend on casual bookings to fill these. In the next period no full-time child can be accepted because some of the sessions are occupied. This is not a good use of resources and is poor childcare. The area is a minefield because apart from financial consideration it is difficult to settle a child who only attends one or two sessions each week.

Juggling the waiting list becomes a constant preoccupation with some managers whether their systems are computerised or not and can become a major source of stress.

PLANNING EVENTS

A work plan for the centre should be set up and take the form of an annual calendar drawn up to include:

- religious festivals/cultural events/social events
- children's vacations
- staff vacations

- seasonal outings, e.g. panto, picnics
- nursery to school transitions creating spaces
- advertising for children's vacancies
- curriculum planning/arrangements periods.

DISPLAY SYSTEM

The following materials must be displayed:
- parents' notices
- weekly menus
- fire exits
- fire drill procedure
- food allergy notices for individual children in the kitchen with photos and treatments if appropriate
- skin allergy notices for individual children in the bathroom
- daily events board – for staff communication.
- public liability insurance.

One thing that is desirable but not essential to display is photographs of staff with names and roles.

GOOD PRACTICE

It is simple to devise work plans and display these in the nursery to facilitate routine tasks, e.g. cleaning routines (see Samples 18, 19 and 20 on the CD-Rom).

In the nursery

Sample 29 gives a standard list of displayed information. It is important that the manager reviews these displays regularly as they can easily deteriorate and create a poor image. This task can either be structured into the manager's week or delegated as part of a job-enhancement system.

See Sample 29 on CD-Rom.

(Note: These displays are in addition to normal vocational displays, e.g. parents' noticeboard, children's work displays etc.)

BOOKS SYSTEMS

Books, such as the incident book, should be kept in the office and treated with respect. Whether any entries are made or not, the book should be signed off each week at a time arranged and noted.

The books themselves are simple. They require only the date and time, an entry and signature and, of course, the checking signature. For example:

| 21 June 2004 | Fire Alarms Tested | Signed: | *Jackie Sadek* |
| 10.00 a.m. | Found in good order | Checked: | *Elizabeth Sadek* |

ROTA

If staff work in shifts, a formula for cover will need to be agreed. It is important to remember that it is not essential that staff work the same times each day. In fact, it is empowering for staff to jointly arrange their own rota and this task can be safely delegated to them – although periodic checks should be made to ensure equity and avoid scapegoating, either intentionally or otherwise.

GOOD PRACTICE

It will develop trust among staff if they feel they are allowed to allocate duty times to fit in with their family commitments.

Use of technology

Another challenge for nursery managers lies in the use of technology to process and transmit information. A large number of software packages has been developed for nursery management and these can be run on standard personal computers. There are several excellent packages for staff who feel confident with computers. These programmes may prove helpful once there are over 20 children; below that number a manual system is as easy to manage – unless the computer can be used for other nursery activities.

Whilst computers are always useful in any organisation which is subject to constant change, a computer does become essential if, and only if, it will perform one or more of the following functions for you:

- increase the efficiency of the organisation (and so reduce the costs)
- improve the quality (and perhaps the quantity) of the service
- give staff more control over the work load and not fully occupy their time.

Many nursery managers have found that computers are worthwhile and today many benefit from having at least a rudimentary computer, but it is still perfectly possible to run an efficient and top-quality childcare service without one. As a high-expenditure item, it is a good idea to consider carefully before choosing to purchase a computer.

Remember also the GIGO effect: 'Garbage in, garbage out'. It is wholly unwise to put anything onto computer unless the manual version is already working well and is fully understood by the personnel involved.

If you are seriously considering making the transition from a paper-based system to software, the best advice is to write down and be clear in your own mind about exactly what you want the programme to *do for you*. In Chapters 1, 2 and 3, we examined the type of records that might be kept on computer. Once you have written your ideas down, go along to nurseries in the area where appropriate software is in use and ask to have it demonstrated. Only then can you make an informed decision.

If dealing with the computer takes staff away from spending time with the children then it is not a good investment.

Marketing the nursery

As we have already noted, it is important to try to keep the nursery places fully occupied.

In one local authority recently, information was sought on how parents had heard of daycare services for under-eights. The breakdown of responses was as follows:

Friends	2262	Yellow Pages	9
Local school	1300	Leaflets	8
Neighbours	914	Notices	8
Health visitor	642	Childminder	7
Public library	538	Word of mouth	7
Family member	401	Phoning	5
EYDCP (CIS)	252	Shop ads	5
Education department	171	Nursery itself	4
Newspapers	110	Parish magazines	4
National Childbirth Trust (NCT)	30	Work	4
Sports centres	23	Parent and toddler group	2
Borough/district councils	16	Community care	2
Childminders' group	14	Playgroup	2
Church	13	Other	10
Doctor's surgery	10		

If the response to the research is to be taken seriously then marketing should be designed accordingly and the nursery clearly needs take steps to make a lot of friends.

GOOD PRACTICE

Care should be taken with the marketing budget as it can be an extremely expensive item. The research indicates that simply buying newspaper advertising space is not effective. Nothing replaces personal recommendation. Local service providers, school teachers and health visitors are always happy to recommend quality provision, and strong links should be forged with these professionals.

Fashion among parents will have some effect on the marketing techniques to be used. It is undoubtedly true that parents are making more and more demands on nurseries to 'educate' the pre-school child. This is what the Americans call the 'push-down' effect. Academic expectations are being pushed down the age groups so that demands for achievements once made on adolescents are now being made on younger children. In this, parents are supported by Ofsted and the Qualifications and Curriculum Authority.

The research indicates that the quality of the service is the single most important selling point as most recommendation come from existing users. Parents are – quite rightly – not ready to trust advertisements in this vital area.

CHILDREN'S INFORMATION SERVICE (CIS)

Most EYDCP have appointed CIS officers. Information on all children's services, free at point of delivery, is available. This service will include details of early years provision in the area. It is in the centre's interest to make contact with the local CIS and confirm the details of the centre being issued to enquirers.

Strategic planning in early years provision

The systems for planning work that have been considered in this chapter are one part of the overall plan of the nursery. They take into account those aspects of the organisation that are quantifiable.

There is another form of planning that can be described using a term borrowed from management theory – *strategic planning*. This describes a level of planning in which most successful businesses engage.

Strategy refers to a system of objectives and plans, as well as the allocation of resources to achieve these objectives and plans. *Financial planning* is only one part of the process of allocation of resources designed to achieve the organisation's objectives. Strategic planning takes into account factors other than the financial, some of which are non-quantifiable and some of which require the exercise of judgement.

SWOT ANALYSIS

SWOT analysis is a useful method of assessing a tricky situation. This technique is often used at times of change when contemplating expansion or contraction, or before embarking on a marketing exercise or some other large expenditure.

In brief, the idea is to consider the **S**trengths and **W**eaknesses of the internal organisation and compare these with the **O**pportunities and **T**hreats to the organisation from outside.

- *Strengths:* internal factors likely to enhance performance, e.g. well-trained staff, a good location, good contacts with local schools, healthy waiting lists.
- *Weaknesses:* internal factors likely to hold back performance, e.g. high fixed costs, long-term staff illness, poor Ofsted report.
- *Opportunities:* external factors that could favour the organisation, e.g. introduction of pre-school voucher funding, a new housing development nearby, closure of a competitor.
- *Threats:* external factors which could be detrimental to the organisation, e.g. the opening of a work-based nursery nearby taking children who were formerly regular attenders, loss of parking spaces.

Although this type of analysis is usually undertaken by management groups, it can be used to good effect in the nursery staff team as the basis for a focused discussion or to assist decision making on such questions as:

- Should the nursery open a baby room?
- Should the nursery offer the extended day?

THE STRATEGIC PLAN

To be acceptable to the nursery, a decision not only has to be affordable, it also has to fit in with the strategic plan of the organisation. In business, continued existence is the ultimate objective – the organisation has to plan to achieve that because it is engaged in fierce competition both for markets and resources. The strategic plan has to take into account the objectives of the organisation, some of which are expressed in terms of financial return or in market growth. The plan is based on a careful analysis of the relative strengths and weaknesses of the organisation, and an assessment of the opportunities in the markets open to it.

The strategic plan has to be based on more than the access to and control of financial resources. Personnel, supplies, market opportunities and technological change all need to be considered. Indeed, the organisation may also have social and psychological objectives that have to be taken into account.

The typical strategic plan sets out where it sees the organisation going over the next ten years or so.
■ In which areas will it expand?
■ In which will it contract?
■ Will it rely on internal growth or will it resort to growth through acquisition?
■ Which parts of the company will be sold off?
The plan has to satisfy the financial objectives, the marketing objectives and the social objectives of those making the decisions on behalf of the company.

There are many techniques designed to assist companies in their strategic planning. One of the earliest of these was that developed and marketed by the Boston Consulting Group. Their approach was to clarify each area of the business on the basis of its relative market and technological competitiveness and the potential growth rate of that part of the business. Each area of the business, each segment, was classified as either a 'star', a 'dog', a 'cash flow' or a 'question mark'.

These classifications would be important when it came to making investment decisions. An investment proposal from a division classified as a 'dog' would be most unlikely to receive approval, this signifying an area of the business in which competitively one was at a disadvantage and where there was little or no market growth possibilities. However, an investment proposed by a division in the 'star' category would stand a good chance of being approved. The investment would have satisfied the question 'Does it fit in with the strategic plan?' It would, of course, still be necessary for the particular investment to satisfy the financial hurdle, e.g. to show a positive net present value.

Many other strategic planning techniques have been developed, one being that of the consulting group 'Organisation'. This, as with the Boston Group approach, recognises that in a large and organisationally complex company, the resource allocation process will need to be in two stages:

- one is the formation of plans leading to the provisional allocation of capital at group level
- the second is the approval of individual investment decisions.

This section of the chapter is emphasising the first of these stages; there is more to capital investment appraisal than selecting between a number of unrelated investment proposals.

The Organisation approach is to divide a business into what are called 'strategic business units'. It is to these units that the headquarters of the company will allocate investment funds. The units are analysed and placed into categories on the basis of their market attractiveness and their competitive strengths in these markets, a not dissimilar approach to that of the Boston Group.

CASE STUDY

A private pre-prep school, in an attempt to improve its falling rolls (when it changed hands), had its whole future secured by taking two steps:

1. opening a pre-nursery group for 2–3-year-olds (who then stayed on to 13 years)
2. opening an out-of-school care service before and after school each day and providing holiday cover.

By these two strategies, the school became a possible childcare solution for working parents.

The new head met a local need and he also saved his school!

Planning can be divided into two types:

- top-down planning, and
- bottom-up planning.

Basically, strategic planning is top-down, but it should be a process that takes into account the views of the units being planned. The overall capital budget of a company must be based on strategic consideration; it cannot just be a selection of individual investment proposals that have come forward from the 'bottom up'. The capital investment plan of a company is part only of a larger planning exercise.

PLANNING AND OBJECTIVES

The first stage in setting up any early years project is to establish its main objective(s) in line with policies and procedures. For example, this might be 'to provide quality childcare at an affordable price'. The objectives are the starting point for project planning as they provide the lead for subsequent policy decisions, such as who the potential users of the facility will be, the ages of the children, the criteria for admission and so on. The objectives may be social or economic and, where the operation is set up as a separate legal entity, these will form a key part of the constitution. It is vital that they are clear, unambiguous statements and are fully agreed by the management team. Clear directives at an early planning stage may avoid crisis management situations occurring at the operational stage of the project.

It is likely that the parents/carers (as potential users) will be involved during these initial planning stages – indeed, in the case of a work-based or community nursery they may be members of the steering committee. Incorporating their views early on will ensure that the future service provided will reflect their needs. A survey of potential users may be required at this point to assess their needs accurately. Provision should be made in the management structure to allow all users to:

- have access to information
- to participate in meetings, and
- to have a forum for expressing their views on the service provided, once the project is up and running, as required under the 1989 Children Act and the National Standards.

The involvement of the users is important to the success of the project, as it is essential that the childcare provision reflects and responds to the needs of the child and of the parent/carer. Childcare should not be regarded in isolation from the family, home and culture. Quality childcare provision can play an important role in the development of the child and, therefore, parents/carers need to be consulted about the type of service being provided.

KEYS TO GOOD PRACTICE

- Involve the parents in the decision-making processes of the nursery.
- Devise an annual programme for marketing the nursery.
- Set up and systemise administrative systems in accordance with the needs of the 1989 Children Act and National Standards.
- In the event of an accident, record it in the proper manner and ask the parent/carer to sign to acknowledge that they have been notified of the accident.
- Ensure that a copy of the local authority procedures for child protection is available for staff use.
- Ensure that display items are in good order and that the care of such items is systemised.
- Develop procedures to measure the performance of the nursery.
- Keep by the telephone a card index with details of information that might be needed quickly.

---

8 RECRUITING STAFF FOR QUALITY EARLY YEARS PROVISION

> **What this chapter covers:**
> - initiating the selection process
> - interviewing and choosing staff
> - induction and mentoring of new staff
> - teams, team roles, team building and team conflict.

This chapter is about what is, in most managers' opinion, the most important task they ever perform – the one to be undertaken with the greatest care, with the clearest head and with the most intelligence. This is the task of choosing the staff, settling them in, supporting their work and making them into real team members.

It is rare, but not unknown, to be in a position to choose all staff from scratch. It is more likely that new members will be joining an existing team, and for this reason some suggestions about team roles are included. Fortunately, their existing interpersonal expertise makes this work much less daunting for new childcare managers than for many others.

Initiating the selection process

Selection is often thought of in its narrowest context, i.e. using techniques that enable the selector to choose one candidate rather than another for a particular post. This view is restrictive as it places emphasis on the needs of the selectors at the expense of those of the candidates, who also require information on which they can base their decision as to whether they wish to accept the post being offered.

To satisfy both these aspects, selection needs to be viewed as a two-way process that involves both the giving and receiving of information, so that the post is filled by the applicant who:
- is most capable of satisfying the requirements of the post (preferably in both the short and long term)
- will fit into the environment and will perform well with existing colleagues
- wishes to accept the post based on knowledge and impressions gained and their own assessment of how they will fit into the organisation and contribute to its objectives.

By its very nature, the childcare profession is labour intensive. There can be little argument concerning the importance of the contribution that staff make to the centre's level of performance. The standards accepted by staff become the standards of the institution and these directly affect the satisfaction of parents.

In addition, the future quality of the service and life of the children will be governed directly by the ability of staff to cope with the demands of any future changes and to provide quality role models for the children. For this reason the selection of staff is one of the most important decisions made by those in management positions within nurseries.

Unfortunately those making appointments are often so busy that they have little time for reflection and make their decisions intuitively on small samples of behaviour that are haphazard and in no way serve as indicators of future performance.

To reduce the risks involved in selection there is a need for a system that supports those having to make decisions by presenting them with the best information possible.

However, before we explore selection systems, it is worthwhile pointing out that there is no such thing as an 'off-the-peg' system that can be applied to all situations. The 'closest fit' (between system and situation) can only be achieved by matching it against the particular needs of the unit: its rules, mode of operation, the kind of post under consideration, the particular skills needed and the role the person will occupy in the team.

A further factor worth stressing is that some nurseries will be subject to union or local authority agreements that lay down steps to be followed in promoting or replacing staff. Although there are fewer and fewer in this category, these agreements will influence the systems used and should be checked before the work begins.

Where choice is available, it is worthwhile first considering the advantages and disadvantages of selecting internal or external candidates, as shown below.

Internal candidates
Advantages
   Shows that promotion is possible
   Gives individual staff members an incentive
   You know what you are getting
   The applicant knows what to expect
   Sends a good signal to future external candidates

Disadvantages
   Limits choice of candidates
   May make the organisation inward-looking
   There is no injection of new blood.

External candidates

Advantages
  New skills and experience are brought into the organisation
  Helps to remind others that they have not proved themselves sufficiently

Disadvantages
  It is difficult for one person to have much impact on an existing organisation
  Selection process may result in a candidate who is no better than those
    already in the organisation
  Will mean adjusting the team equilibrium
  May cause dissatisfaction and a view that effort will not be rewarded.

THE PROCESS OF SELECTION

Bearing in mind the constraints already discussed, the process of selection would include the activities shown in the flow diagram opposite.

GOOD PRACTICE

If the nursery is small (fewer than twelve staff) everyone should be consulted in an open manner.

DEFINING THE REQUIREMENTS OF THE POST

The starting point for selection must be some form of study of the post to be filled scoping out the job description and creating a person specification. However, do not be overcome by the many ways available for doing this; allow common sense to prevail.

BACK-UP INFORMATION

The advertisement
The advertisement should be based on the requirements of the person specification and should be designed and worded in such a way that it will appeal to the kind of people you are hoping to attract. At a minimum it should include:

- the title of the post
- an indication of the type of work
- the starting date
- the name of the establishment or department
- the grade and salary
- where and how to obtain further information
- the closing date for applications.

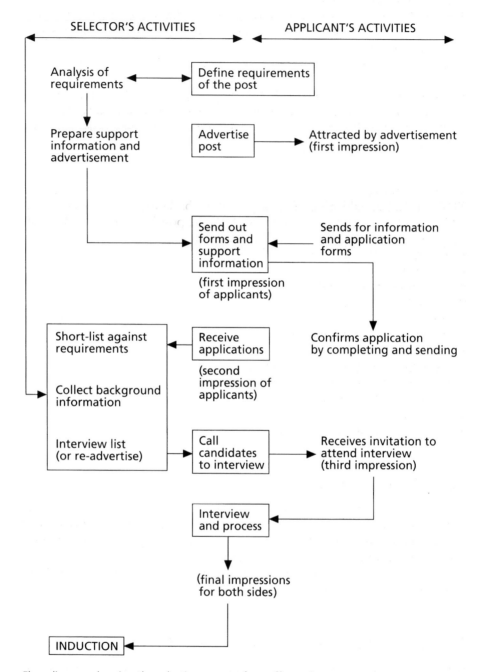

SELECTOR'S ACTIVITIES   APPLICANT'S ACTIVITIES

Analysis of   Define requirements
requirements   of the post

Prepare support   Advertise   Attracted by advertisement
information and   post   (first impression)
advertisement

                       Send out   Sends for information
                       forms and   and application
                       support   forms
                       information

                       (first impression
                       of applicants)

Short-list against   Receive   Confirms application
requirements   applications   by completing and sending

                       (second
                       impression of
Collect background   applicants)
information

Interview list   Call   Receives invitation to
(or re-advertise)   candidates   attend interview
                       to interview   (third impression)

                       Interview
                       and process

                       (final impressions
                       for both sides)

INDUCTION

Flow diagram showing the selection process for staff members

Support information on the post

This will be based on the job requirements and should include information on the conditions under which the duties are to be carried out. This will generally comprise:

- specific detailed requirements of the post in the short and long term, e.g. present duties, future development
- general duties associated with the post, e.g. responsibilities for curriculum, equipment or stock control, for students, for health and safety
- where the post fits into the organisation and where it may lead to in the future.

Support material

This material should be aimed at providing background information on both the authority and the nursery in which the post is located. The kind of information given should generally include:

- description of geographical location
- catchment area and population
- number of nursery and support staff
- description of range of work
- resources
- buildings and accommodation
- transport facilities
- organisational features, if appropriate
- governors (if applicable) or accounting systems
- internal organisation, if appropriate
- conditions of service
- relocation expenses, if appropriate.

ADVERTISING THE POST

To attract the right people, the advertisement must be placed in the most appropriate journal, newspaper or website at the right time. This means that the target audience should be identified as closely as possible before placing the advertisement.

Remember that there are recruiting seasons for some candidates, such as graduates or students direct from training establishments.

SENDING OUT FORMS AND INFORMATION

A policy decision should be taken before placing the advertisement as to whether enquiries for forms should be accompanied by a stamped-addressed envelope (never a bad idea) and whether telephone requests for forms will be accepted or whether the forms can be downloaded directly.

Whichever of the above options is chosen, it is helpful, where possible, to keep a careful record of the number of enquiries for information and forms, and of the names and addresses. These may be useful later should the post be re-advertised. The number of enquiries can be marked against the number of actual applications. These records will also give valuable information as to which advertising vehicle gives the best results for the nursery.

SHORT-LISTING CANDIDATES FROM THE RECEIVED FORMS

Depending on the size of the response, considerable time can be saved if a system has been devised for sifting the information contained in the incoming applications.

Various ranking systems can be used, based on cross-referencing the information and matching it against the personal specifications or requirements of the post. However, care must be taken as all of the information about the candidates will not be available at this stage and the process is limited to considering the following:

- personal details
- education/training
- qualifications
- experience to date
- presentation of information.

If the number of candidates is large and finance is available, preliminary interviews can also be used to prepare the final shortlist of candidates.

COLLECTING BACKGROUND INFORMATION

People vary in the way they check references, with some doing so before the interview and others afterwards.

There are arguments for and against both methods. One thing is clear: considerable tact may be needed, as checking references can have an adverse effect on the careers of external candidates whose employers do not know that they are job hunting.

A further point is that in these days of open references (a reference that has been seen by the subject, or is available to be seen by the subject), research may be necessary to assess the real value of the reference.

CALLING CANDIDATES FOR INTERVIEW

It is worth giving careful thought to the method of calling candidates for interview, as this helps you establish the image of the nursery.

The invitation should include information on the timetable and method of interviewing. It may also include the number of others on the shortlist and should include a map of the location, travelling arrangements and where to obtain accommodation, if this is necessary.

This time/availability can be arranged by phone as long as a paper back-up is also used.

PRESENTATION OF INFORMATION ON THE UNIT/ ORGANISATION

This is the most important stage from the point of view of the candidates, as it is their opportunity to collect information about the unit and its working environment.

It is the period in which they assess whether the information given to them before their arrival represents a true picture of the post and the circumstances under which the duties will be carried out.

The programme of presentation will vary depending upon the number of candidates, the level of the post and the resources available for interviewing.

GOOD PRACTICE

A welcoming programme for the candidates should be arranged. This could include:
- coffee on arrival at the centre
- welcome by the manager or head of department and a general description of the centre and its work
- a tour of the centre with particular emphasis on those parts directly affecting the post on offer
- a meeting with future colleagues
- informal discussions
- formal interviews.

During the important stage many employers also ask candidates to attend the nursery for one or two sessions so that their performance can be observed and their interaction with the children checked.

In respect to very junior posts these arrangements may be modified to avoid overwhelming an anxious applicant.

Interviewing and choosing staff

ESSENTIALS OF GOOD INTERVIEWING

- Every interview has a purpose. Make sure you know what you want from your interview and that you frame your questions accordingly.
- Be prepared. Find out what you can about candidates from their records and make a note of the main questions you wish to put to them.

- Ensure that you are not going to be interrupted and that the interview room is free of distractions.
- Arrange the seating so that you and the candidate can see and hear each other clearly.
- Try to establish a good rapport with the candidate and maintain it throughout. An interview is not an interrogation, nor is it an excuse for playing power games.
- Ask questions that allow candidates to give full answers. Avoid asking too many questions that require only a one-word reply. Also avoid multiple, trick and leading questions that force candidates to answer in the way you want (see the section on 'open' versus 'closed' questions in chapter 9).
- Let candidates do most of the talking and show by voice, facial expression and gesture that you are listening to what they are telling you.

GOOD PRACTICE

Ensure that you have developed your skills in this area prior to embarking on an interview programme. The activity below will give you some practice.
- Should a candidate become upset or hostile, remain calm, objective and detached.
- Avoid any references to the candidate's appearance, sex, age, religion, race or marital status.
- End the interview in the same friendly manner in which it began and, no matter what the nature of the interview, always aim to leave the candidates with their dignity and self-esteem intact.

GOOD PRACTICE

Discussion concerning the childcare needs of the candidate can take place *after* the appointment has been made. If concessionary places are available, information about this arrangement should be set out in the Terms and Conditions of Service.

Activity
This activity is designed to develop your active listening skills. Interviewing and listening skills are essential for a good manager. The next time you are conducting an interview (or appraisal interview) follow these guidelines.
- Have sufficient empathy to create surroundings in which you and the candidate will be comfortable and which are appropriate to the kind of interview you are conducting.
- Decide what you want to achieve from the interview in advance and plan it properly.
- Leave yourself time and freedom from interruptions so that you can concentrate on the interviewee's problems and not your own.

- Recognise and acknowledge any prejudices you may harbour and keep them out of the interview, to the best of your ability.
- Do not accept everything the interviewee tells you at face value. Probe evasions and clichés, and examine half-truths.
- Be patient. Do not interrupt. Let the interviewee finish before asking the next question.
- Be tolerant. You may not like what interviewees are saying, or even the interviewees themselves, but try to put your personal feelings aside.
- Finally, be comfortable with yourself. The more at ease you are with yourself, the more at ease interviewees will be with you and the more open their answers will be.

SELECTION AND OFFER

Having chosen their favoured candidate, most organisations go through the offer and acceptance stage before dismissing the other candidates. This is done in order that a follow-up offer can be made immediately to the second candidate if the first refuses the post. A contract of employment (see Sample 40 on CD-Rom) should be offered and, if possible, talked over with new colleagues. One copy should be retained by the nursery and one by the staff member.

GOOD PRACTICE

It is courteous at this stage for the manager or senior member of staff to thank the unsuccessful candidates and wish them well in the future. Constructive feedback on interview performance should be offered.

Induction and mentoring of new staff

Obviously, your system of appointment should not end with the appointment having been made. Steps should be taken to get the selected candidate eased into the requirements of the post and settled into the nursery. You will have (hopefully) appointed someone whose ethics, values and performance mesh with those of the organisation. Recognise that:
- the appointee now needs to be established and consolidated on a foundation of mutual respect and trust
- it takes time and communication to establish rapport
- this new relationship is crucial to the success of your team and it is therefore worth investing time and effort in the early stages.

It is also worth investing time and effort into a good induction programme (see Sample 51), as this will meet important objectives, such as gaining greater employee loyalty, developing a stronger managerial base for future promotions or ending gender and racial inequalities. Later on, you may be expecting your new recruit to participate in recruiting and developing their own replacement as they move up the career ladder, so it is important to establish solid foundations.

Induction generally falls into two parts. The period between the appointment and taking up of the post should be used for providing information on timetables, curriculum matters and other general information. A visit to the centre is useful for giving this information if it can be arranged. For the initial period in post, junior members of staff can be placed under the general guidance of a colleague upon whom they can call for help with minor problems. This is known as *mentoring*.

Large nurseries or daycare centres may have formal induction programmes covering the first weeks in the post. Alternatively, you may have to invent a programme for your new member of staff and this is best done *together* with that new member of staff.

In the nursery

With any new team member, it is important – on Day One – to outline the expectations, and limits, of both the individual concerned and the existing team and to revisit the contract of employment. One good way is to write down what you expect of the new employee and, perhaps more importantly, what your new recruit can (and is prepared to) offer. Go gently on formalising this – some people balk at the idea of having too many demands put upon them in the early stages. In any case, this 'agreement' will, obviously, change and be superseded as the new staff member settles into the job. Ideally, your relationship is going to be a long-term one. Use an appropriate job description for this purpose.

See Samples 42–47 on the CD-Rom.

GOOD PRACTICE

Try to put yourself into the new person's shoes and anticipate their needs. It is natural for the new recruit to suffer from a feeling of isolation at first in the new environment. This is where a mentor becomes invaluable.

A mentor is someone who can challenge, support, advise, motivate and encourage your new member of staff. It must be someone who understands the work and believes in the potential of the new recruit. A mentor will provide a safe harbour for the new team member – a space to ask questions, think out loud and make mistakes without feeling embarrassed or quashed. A good mentor will view the new recruit objectively and give constructive feedback along with general guidance.

In the nursery

The mentor could be you – the nursery managers – but it is generally more effective if it is a colleague who is more senior than the new recruit (but not intimidating) or who is at the same level but who has been in the job for long enough to know the ropes. If the mentor is also the manager of the recruit, the recruit will be so anxious to please that they may find it difficult to ask unguarded questions. Similarly, do not put a new recruit into the care of a mentor who is already a friend of the new recruit (for instance, knew them at college) as true friends are rarely objective enough about each other. Use Samples 58–60 (which can be adapted for your own purposes) as a system for mentoring the skills of the new staff member.

See Samples 58–60 on the CD-Rom.

Teams, team roles and team building

The development or building of a team reflects the path taken in the development of any group. The life cycle of all teams means that every team will go through the same stages as it evolves:
- it forms
- it storms
- it norms
- it performs.

It is the manager/leader's role to move the team from 'forming' to 'performing' as quickly as possible. It should be borne in mind that, like the children's 'stages', the process can be quick or slow but all the stages will have to be gone through – and, of course, the manager/leader is part of this dynamic process.

THE FORMING STAGE

While in the forming stage members' behaviour to each other will be as follows
- showing extra politeness
- smiling a lot (but not laughing)
- avoiding any contentious issues
- assessing each other personally
- assessing each other professionally.

This behaviour is what has been described by other theorists as 'sniffing out' the ground rules.

The leader/manager's guidelines for action at this stage are to provide:
- venues for small social events, e.g. coffee, after-work drinks
- opportunities/access for small chats/interactions.

This stage may take some time but it may not, however, be over when the first conflict appears. The conflict is a sign that the end of the stage is approaching.

THE STORMING STAGE

While in the storming stage members' behaviour to each other will be as follows:
- open or hidden display of dissent
- no longer smiling at each other
- pre-occupied with administration, form filling, rule checking
- challenging who gives and takes orders
- generally challenging
- a power struggle in process
- establishing a pecking order.

The leader/manager's guidelines for this stage are to:
- initiate damage limitation, i.e. do not allow staff conflict to be obvious to parents or children
- keep open communication with all members
- listen to everyone
- resolve conflict in a professional manner
- arrange group and sub-group meetings
- keep the goals in everyone's mind
- avoid additional tasks, e.g. appraisal etc.

This stage must be moved along, although sometimes groups get stuck, causing stress and high staff turnover – which, of course, means we have to start all over again: back to the new group and the 'forming'.

The end of this stage is reached when members begin to solve their own problems.

THE NORMING STAGE

While in the norming stage members' behaviour to each other is as follows:
- consensus and co-operation emerges
- the words 'we' or 'team' may be used
- begin to make friendships
- evidence of confidence in self and others begins to appear
- the atmosphere is lightened.

The leader/manager's guidelines for this stage are to:
- promote staff involvement in planning, e.g. curriculum work in goal setting
- continue with open, friendly approach to all.

THE PERFORMING STAGE

While in the performing stage members' behaviour to each other is as follows:
- begin to deliver quality care
- take responsibility for self and team

- will now engage in appraisals
- take pride in achievements.

The leader/manager's guidelines for this stage are to:
- relax a bit about team monitoring
- get on with other tasks assuming support of team
- begin to start the staff development and continuing professional development (CPD) process.

When a team disbands for whatever reason it is the leader/manager's job to create closure, to review reward and celebrate the team by some social gesture.

If the team has finished on a high – a good Ofsted report, for instance – this is an easy task, but if the team dissolves when there is little to celebrate it is still vital that the manager contrives to create closure.

We often comment on teams by saying that 'the whole is greater than the sum of the parts' without really stopping to consider what that statement means. The importance of having an effective team in a childcare context cannot be overestimated. We will now explore a management model that can assist the manager in putting together a good 'whole' – a good team, greater than the sum of its parts.

The concept of 'team' can be quite elusive: it is evident that people many function as a team without being part of a working group. Conversely, people may belong to the same working group without constituting a team. The essence of a team is that its members form a co-operative association through a division of labour that best reflects the contribution that each can make towards the common objective. The members do not need to be present at the same place and at the same time to enable the team to function.

THE CHARACTERISTICS OF A TEAM

It is helpful to explore the characteristics of a team. In any organisation a good team will:

- work together
- share a common aim
- co-operate with others
- share/communicate/support between its members
- have motivation for the task in hand
- have catalytic relationships so that new ideas are extended
- be committed to the task and the team
- be comprised of members who each understand their own role in the team and are reliable in it
- complete the task.

Clearly if a team does not or cannot fulfil these criteria then it will not be a good team and will not best serve the needs of the organisation. Management theorists have, therefore, spent time and effort working out how and why teams work.

TEAM ROLE MODELS

A British theorist, Meredith Belbin, spent many years observing teams at work and redesigning these teams to see if productivity improved. From this work he built a *team role model* (1981), which identifies how individuals are likely to work within a team and how to put together combinations of individuals to get the best results.

Most teams are commonly made up of members holding particular roles. They are there by virtue of the position or responsibilities they represent. No overall sense of design governs the composition of the group which, in human terms, is little more than a random collection of people with as wide a spread of human foibles and personality characteristics as one might expect to find in the population at large.

Nevertheless it is clear that the compatibility of members of the team is crucial to its effectiveness. The question of the interaction of members within a team becomes more important the more often a team meets. It is a subject of no less importance than whether members of a team are qualified to be Nursery Assistants or Officers-in-Charge. The problem is that human compatibility is more difficult to assess than technical competence. Belbin's experiments and fieldwork give some leads on how the subject of compatibility within teams might be approached.

Belbin's studies showed that there are eight 'team roles' that people will assume in a group, as listed below.

Resource Investigator (RI): the team member who explores and reports on ideas or developments outside the group; good at making external contacts and at conducting negotiations; usually outgoing and relaxed, with a strong inquisitive sense; always ready to see the possibilities inherent in anything new.

Co-ordinator (Co): the person who controls the way the team moves forward towards its objectives by making the best use of the team's resources; good at recognising where the team's strengths and weaknesses lie; good at ensuring that the best use is made of the potential of each member of the team; sometimes acts as the chairperson of the group but need not be the official leader of the team; this person talks easily, listens carefully and basically trusts people.

Shaper (SH): this person shapes the way in which the team effort is applied, directing attention to the setting of objectives and priorities and seeking to impose some shape or pattern on group discussion and on the outcome of group activities; anxious, dominant and extrovert, full of nervous energy, the shaper is outgoing, emotional, impulsive and impatient but has nervous energy and commitment which ensure that the team remains task-orientated and able to achieve.

Completer/finisher (CF): protects the team from mistakes of both commission and omission, actively searches for aspects of work which require a more than usual degree of attention and maintains a sense of urgency within the team; has a sense of concern with order and purpose and usually has good self-control and strength of character; a strong concern for detail and a tendency to check everything personally to make sure that nothing has been overlooked.

Implementer (IMP): turns concepts and plans into working procedures; plenty of self-discipline, combined with realistic, practical common sense; a practical organiser, translating policy decisions into easily understood procedures, then getting on with the work. This person likes structure and order and dislikes mess and chaos. Because of an essentially practical orientation, many nursery nurses are naturally in the implementer role.

Monitor Evaluator (ME): this team member is particularly good at analysing problems and evaluating ideas and suggestions with an objective mind and the ability to think critically; able to analyse huge quantities of data; this person is most likely to identify the flaws in an argument and to stop the team from committing itself to a misguided project.

Team Worker (TW): this is often the most sensitive member of the group, very aware of the needs and worries of the other team members and is able to sense undercurrents; a good communicator; a good listener; he or she promotes unity and harmony so that the team, as a whole, works better when the Team Worker is there – things are different if he or she is absent.

Plant (PL): this team member contributes by putting forward new ideas and strategies; the most imaginative and intelligent member of the team, most likely to come up with radical new approaches; the person who is likely to provide the solution to a problem.

Belbin concluded that good teams would be much easier to form in organisations if thought were given to the team role composition of natural working groups. In practice, however, there are a multitude of reasons why well-balanced teams are unlikely to form spontaneously. People are often picked for working groups because it is sensed that they have characteristics akin to those who are already there. So redundancies in some team roles will be associated with shortages in others. At higher levels of responsibility similar team role types are found because the organisation favours and rewards with promotion those with particular styles of approach.

One of the prime obstacles to many managers utilising a team role approach is that an unchangeable staffing structure precludes entry into the team by the most suitable individuals. This raises the question of how a good team can be formed in a nursery that is not recruiting or likely to transfer people from the jobs they currently hold. However, if there is any room for manoeuvre, there are potential benefits for managers of the team role model, as outlined below.

ISSUES IN RECRUITMENT TO THE TEAM USING THE BELBIN MODEL

When a new staff member is being sought, what sort of person should the nursery look for? The orthodox, almost reflex response, is for a nursery to search for someone who fits the image of those who are already there. Fewer problems then arise in mutual adjustment between the newcomer and his or her established colleagues. However, in team role terms the more fundamental need is for someone who will fill the team role gap in the group. This cannot be ascertained without completing a team role inventory of colleagues and examining what is missing. Once this has been done, a personal specification can be drawn up of the general shape of the candidate the nursery needs to recruit. The interview now becomes directed towards the key question that the selectors will be posing to themselves: how far does the candidate match the personal specification?

INTERNAL RESHUFFLING

The second immediate benefit of using team role concepts relates to internal postings. Managers have reported advantages in being able to make bolder moves than they would otherwise contemplate through confidence that the appointee will contribute the team role that is lacking. This occurs typically where the experience that the incoming staff member brings with her or him is not altogether appropriate but his or her natural orientation and behaviour more than compensates for any deficiency in technical knowledge. (The converse point is also important: internal postings that suggest themselves for technical reasons could be questioned once the implications of the move in team role terms have been explored.)

PROTECTING VIABLE PARTNERSHIPS

A common mistake is to underestimate the dynamic factors that bind together the smallest team of all. Pairings of proven effectiveness (such as Nursery Officer-in-Charge and her Deputy) are often broken up to fill managerial gaps (e.g. to cover maternity leave in another nursery) or even as well-intentioned acts of management development, with little realisation of how much the interdependence of these two people contributes to the running of a successful unit. (In industry, successful twosomes are more stable in top management than on the way up. A Chairman and a Managing Director who establish a good working relationship maintain it to the benefit of the enterprise as a whole. In contrast, any junior executive pair that does well will seldom be seen as anything other than two able individuals.)

In the nursery
Theory says that each individual will always fulfil the same role in any team – obviously it is helpful for your own use to know what that role is. Use of an appropriate questionnaire will help determine which team roles you and your team members will occupy.
  See Sample 61 on the CD-Rom.

TEAM BUILDING

Establishing the right climate in which well-designed teams can form and flourish is the foundation stone on which more effective teamwork in the future can be built. Only then does it become possible to explore the many questions raised by trying to create an optimum combination of people. The merits of each potential member can be raised in terms of what they technically can contribute and the roles they are likely to play in the group that is being formed. Once this process starts one finds that some people have more to contribute than others irrespective of what it is they have to offer. Designing a team engenders a search for individuals who are good examples of their type. Team building is an art in that everyone is different and combinations of different people are not wholly predictable.

Once the team has been put together, the free exchange of opinions in that team – whether it be in industry or in the childcare service – is vital for the success of that team. There are enormously pleasurable aspects of team work such as succeeding as a team and sharing praise. Where criticism and correction are necessary they need to be offset by praise and thanks. The people around you will blossom or wither depending on the balance between the encouragement and the criticism that you give to them.

For a manager, the ability to support and lead a group is critical not just to the well-being of the staff concerned and for the organisation, but also to give you enormous invaluable support and strength.

Team work is about *trust,* giving staff the opportunity to develop decision-making skills. Good team players give their staff the facts and let them have a say in decisions that affect them.

Conflict can arise from many areas in early years settings:

Mnemonic identifying origins of conflict in staff teams – PLUS and MINUS
Policies in the Centre
Leadership style in the Centre
Unwritten value systems
Structure of the Centre

Administrative anomalies in job descriptions
No staff time all together for breaks and meetings
Disparity in qualifications among staff

Moving on – staff leaving after only short service
Individual value systems
Negative attitudes in staff and sometimes parents
Unconventional holders of power
Shift systems.

Some of the conflicts can be solved easily; others are more intransigent. We consider each conflict in turn below.

ORIGINS OF CONFLICT IN THE NURSERY TEAM

However hard the manager works to build the team and support it through its development, conflict still arises in every early years setting. Sometimes the conflict is dysfunctional, more often mildly irritating. Some theorists argue that it is actually a positive feature of nursery life – the positive aspects commonly quoted are by Rodd (1994).

Positive aspects of conflict	Negative aspects of conflict
Indicates lively involvement	Creates poor morale
Refutes 'burn out'	High staff turnover
Reduces complacency	High absentee rate
Pinpoints issues in the staff team	Poor staff development.

Details of the sources of conflict listed in the mnemonic are described, alongside suggested solutions.

Policies in the centre
Although often devised by the staff who are expected to adhere to them, policies frequently attract hostility from individuals within the group. For example, some staff simply do not feel that parents should be treated as partners nor that we are all equal. They will, of course, pay lip service to the policies but they will experience discomfort in welcoming parents at any

time in the working day, and may be unhappy at working with a disabled colleague although very nurturing to any child in their care with the same disability.

Suggested solution
1. This is a clear case for staff development and team building.
2. During the appraisal interviews, identify training/skills gaps and encourage the staff members to avail themselves of such opportunities.
3. Fix a time for feedback.
4. Where policies are clearly being blatantly ignored a direct confrontation is unavoidable. This matter should be dealt with privately and the staff member treated firmly but with respect. Record the incident for inclusion in the next appraisal exercise.

Leadership style
The leadership style demonstrated by the manager will not automatically suit all staff. For example, inexperienced staff may seek directives, simply not being sufficiently confident to know what to do in every day-to-day situation. Others will bitterly resent the same approach, which they perceive as interference or 'bossiness'.

The reverse is true: overly permissive, laissez-faire leaders are seen as accepting poor quality work and risk losing the respect of staff and parents alike.

Suggested solution
1. Develop an open style and share information.
2. Do not be self-serving – take your turn at doing the dirty jobs.
3. Respect others – children, parents and staff vocational and support staff alike.
4. Be assertive not aggressive with everyone.
5. Develop skills of problem solving.

Unwritten value systems
Unwritten and unclear value systems exist in many centres (the 'Somewhere way' described in Chapter 4) and create difficulties for all new staff at whatever level they are appointed. They will take sometime to access the 'Somewhere way' of doing things and indeed may leave before they ever do, claiming they never 'fitted in' and having their confidence shaken in the process.

Suggested solution
1. If the unwritten value systems are valid then *write them down* or write the valid ones down and attempt to extinguish the less well-founded ones. Incorporate them into the mission statement and the procedures – acknowledge these unwritten values.
2. Attach all new staff to a mentor. Write a clear task description for the

mentoring role. Arrange for mentor and appointee to report together on their experience within one month of the start date of the new members. Review later if needed.

Structures

Structures within full daycare quite rightly reflect the needs of the children and are organised into separate spaces accommodating small groups of children being cared for by even smaller groups of staff. These staff do not easily mix; they develop allegiances within their own circle. So 'Babies' staff don't always agree with the 'Tweenies' people who don't see eye to eye with 'Toddlers' workers who have no time at all for the teachers in the 'Big school'.

Suggested solution
1. Junior staff and students should be rotated across all areas of the centre to facilitate their study and widen their experience in occupational choice.
2. Senior staff in all areas should be encouraged to develop team building skills within their teams and to take responsibility for their relationship with each other.
3. Develop a senior staff forum so that there is a place for meeting and planning and because this creates alternative bonding.

Administrative systems

Where administrative systems provide a poor or badly written job description, person specification or none at all (in the worst case scenarios), staff at all levels are unsure of what exactly their role might be.

Suggested solution
This is perhaps the easiest problem to solve.
1. Undertake a review of all job descriptions using the samples (42–47) on the CD-Rom and the appraisal methods described; negotiate where differences are evident and keep the items on the review list until the issue is resolved and everyone knows their role.
2. Fix a time for review and/or feedback. Review job descriptions annually.

No staff time

This means things like staff having no time together without children to supervise for casual communication over breaks or lunch. Planning and staff meeting must be scheduled in their 'own' time. For many working women, who comprise the main staff pool for nurseries, the time they are not working is by no means their 'own' time.

Suggested solution
1. Ensure that staff contracts include the requirement to attend planning

meetings at agreed times outside nursery hours. Be specific about the need to meet, how and when they are planned and the importance of everyone's contribution.

2. Encourage staff to take time in lieu and to accumulate this time to a certain agreed level.

3. Where you are changing existing practice, build this item into the appraisal process.

Disparity in the qualifications held by staff

This can cause occupational skills to be challenged. Where different conditions of service still exist (for example, between teaching and care staff) resentment is often experienced – particularly where a nursery officer may feel herself to possess more appropriate competences than her teaching colleague who is paid more, enjoys shorter days, longer holidays and who never works shifts.

There may also be some distrust between staff who have the same conditions of service but different types of qualifications – one perhaps college-based (BTEC/NNEB) and the other work-based (NVQ).

Suggested solution

1. Prepare an organisational chart illustrating the differing roles and responsibilities of differing members of staff and indicate where these support and complement each other (Sample 60).

2. Involve teaching staff with in-house training in their area of expertise, e.g. the foundation curriculum, progressing to 'big school'.

3. Involve all staff in team-building playing to the strengths of each.

4. Revisit job description of the colleague who is suffering most – suggest enhancement, further training or even relocation within the nursery, e.g. retrain as Health and Safety Officer, SENCO, NVQ Assessor.

Moving on

Moving on refers to the situation where staff only stay in post for short periods. The high staff turnover endemic in nursery work results in an ever-changing team membership, which is therefore constantly held at the 'storming' phase of their team development.

Suggested solution

1. There is none! This simply has to be accepted.

2. Avoid placing new staff in a 'stormy' team. High drop-out exists in all nurseries at all times. The drop-out is simply a function of the age (18– 25) and gender (female) of the dominant group of workers in this area. These women train and then move to the first job (where they are not perceived as students); move to be near partners; take maternity leave; return to work, maybe part-time; take second maternity leave from which they do not return immediately.

A common life pattern is then to become a childminder or voluntary worker in their children's school and to reappear in the workforce aged thirty or so to become stable part-time, and then full-time, members of staff. This may involve six or seven different appointments in just so many years. Therefore the strategy is to support and encourage young staff but to be sufficiently flexible to value them for their youth and vitality and recognise that they will move on but take on, to their own children and others later, the lessons learned in their training, as well as the early good experiences they get in a quality nursery.

Individual value systems

Individual value systems occur where staff members hold strong views on child management (often arising from their own childhood) and cause difficulties through deviating from the usual practices on, say, behaviour management in the centre. Individual value systems often appear around eating habits, e.g., not allowing food or treats until the 'please' and 'thank you' ritual has been observed, not allowing pudding until the main course has been eaten.

Suggested solutions
1. Treat as 'Policies' section above.
2. Involve in team building.

Negative attitudes

Negative attitudes in staff cause them, for example, to not readily develop a professional approach to attending meetings at the centre outside the working day or lead to clockwatching or not volunteering to do anything extra – thereby causing resentment in others.

Negative attitudes are also evident in some parents, causing inexperienced staff considerable discomfort as they are coerced into unprofessional chat and gossip.

Suggested solutions
1. Treat as 'Policies' section above.
2. Involve in team building exercises.

Unconventional holders of power

These exist in many early years centres. Such a person is often a long-serving member of staff who may not hold any legal power. The cook is often a candidate but it can also be a janitor or, in a school, the librarian. This person can be the source of much discomfort, particularly with inexperienced staff who are unsure of their position.

Suggested solution
Treat as for problems around Administration, although the resolution may be more protracted in this instance and may mean more – even daily – meetings to discourage this person from exercising their power over your

staff. Indeed, for some time you may have to absorb their energy yourself in order to protect the team.

Shift systems
In full daycare these cause the nursery to be open from 7 a.m. to 7 p.m. While some staff find the early shift suits their lifestyle this is by no means common. The shift rota often becomes a constant source of resentment and irritation.

Suggested solution
1. Do not delegate writing the rota until you are quite sure the conflict is truly resolved – even where the staff devise the rota themselves weaker members may yield to their more assertive, demanding colleagues.
2. Be very specific on new appointments (and in contracts) about the number of 'earlies' and 'lates' expected. It may be that the rota needs to be worked over a protracted time. The more advance warning and stability in the system, the less the chance of conflict.
3. Be very clear about procedures at the shift interface – e.g. make sure everything needed for the early shift is left ready the night before and the morning staff are not faced with tasks left from their colleagues' hasty departure the night before. These measures will never remove the reluctance of staff to work early shifts but at least it should be clear that equity exists.

The following guidelines will help you to empower your staff.

Delegate, don't dump: delegating is an essential working practice but many managers do not understand what it actually means. If you give away only unpleasant tasks, that is dumping not delegating and your staff will regard it, correctly, as an abuse of power and trust. Delegation is giving something away that can develop someone else's expertise, allowing enough authority to get it done.

Follow through: effective team members remember the promises they make, take the appropriate course of action and let their colleagues know what has been done. If you tell someone that you are going to check on something for them, do it. (If you do not intend to do something, never say you will. Your credibility will go down each time your staff's expectations are not met.) It is a good idea always to carry a notebook when you have a meeting. If you say you are going to do something, let others see that you are writing it down. This signifies that you mean business. Review your notebook regularly and give your staff updates on progress.

Set goals within the team: research has shown that regular goal-setting improves performance more than any other team working technique. Define people's work in terms of goals and objectives that become a basic part of each job description, not something extra or tacked on. To be effective motivators, the goals must be clear and attainable. If possible, each goal should be stated in terms of what the team member must do rather than what the outcome should be. Write everything down.

Encourage everyone to have plans for their future: if your staff feel they cannot move up, they will move out. The possibilities of promotion or of fresh challenges are important motivators. When people feel they can grow in their jobs, they are more likely to work harder at them. Team members should be undergoing training to enable them to fill better positions in the future. (See the use of Continuing Professional Development – CPD – in Chapter 9.)

Minimise stress (see Chapter 9) by ensuring that lines of communication all the way to the top are accessible to everyone, especially the most junior staff. You might have weekly discussions, where group members are able to identify their collective sources of stress. From there, team members can go on to isolate their problems and deal with them.

Give positive feedback to individual members of staff in front of the others. A simple 'Thanks, you did a great job with Mrs Jones – she was very anxious' further boosts morale and makes the team user friendly.

KEYS TO GOOD PRACTICE

- Always look at any person you are about to appoint and ask yourself whether this person is a suitable role model for the children.
- With respect to promotions, all internal applicants should have the courtesy of a private discussion with their line manager whether they are short-listed or not.
- In the event of an internal shortlisted candidate not being appointed, they should be given a feedback interview at the earliest possible opportunity.
- Make sure any new member of staff is introduced to the parents, and their photo and name put on the parents' board *before* the new member arrives. This applies at whatever level the appointment is made.
- Care must be taken when appointing staff to take references from former employees, and to arrange police and health checks (see Sample 62).
- Some police departments charge for making police checks. Small nurseries find this outlay very costly. It is therefore quite in order to ask new members of staff to meet this cost in the first instance, with the monies to be refunded after a specified period of time.
- When a new staff member joins the team, a mentor should be nominated to assist the settling in process.
- A regular appointment should be made with the new team member to check the induction process and update CPD.
- It is important to recognise that any new member joining the team will alter the dynamics within the group. Give thought to the development of the team and to the place of any new member in the team.

9 STAFF DEVELOPMENT IN EARLY YEARS PROVISION

> **What this chapter covers:**
> - staffing and training
> - Continuing Professional Development (CPD)
> - National Vocational Qualifications (NVQs)
> - the appraisal process
> - appraisal interviews
> - self-appraisal.

This chapter is about working with people, about career development, and about guidance and support for staff. It is also about familiarity with the childcare standards to which staff should be performing. It is about recognising where performance falls short of the standards and about taking steps to rectify the situation.

Staffing and training

In the labour-intensive business of childcare, staff are essential to the success of the enterprise. It is good management practice to ensure that staff feel valued and stimulated by their work and have opportunities for training and development. Staff will need to feel they have the ongoing support of the manager or management team, and will require a clear understanding of the aims of the unit (see also sections on motivation in Chapter 5). It is important that the staff feel they are part of a stable and consistent work team, and continuity of staffing has obvious benefits for the children.

GOOD PRACTICE

Establishing a stable and consistent work team can be achieved by:
- establishing pay and conditions of employment that reflect the responsibility undertaken by the carers as well as their skill and abilities
- having a clear staffing policy and selection procedure
- allowing time for staff meetings and regular supervision
- identifying staff training needs and finding training opportunities.

Throughout this chapter we identify issues that lend themselves to in-house staff development.

PRE-SERVICE TRAINING

Pre-service training is offered to young and mature students in further education colleges and in some training agencies. Details of this provision can be found by contacting your local college or library. In recent times the availability of education and training courses has been subject to massive and continuing change so it is important to keep abreast of developments in pre-service training – and managers must develop strategies for this purpose. Information on this can also be obtained from the local Early Years Development and Childcare Partnership (EYDCP).

GOOD PRACTICE

One good method of keeping abreast of developments in training provision is to offer the nursery as a training venue to the local college or agencies. This means you will have access to up-to-date information from the course that you are servicing.

Having students in the nursery does, however, have cost implications because, while their enthusiasm and energy is a welcome addition to the staff group, their training needs must be taken seriously and guidance, instruction and supervision must be made available to them. Nonetheless, having a training unit does bring the advantage that staff are aware of standards required at all times.

It is also important to communicate the role of students to the parents using the centre.

IN-SERVICE TRAINING

Both qualified and unqualified staff are now offered National Vocational Qualifications (NVQs) if the nursery is part of, or has access to, an Assessment Centre. Help with this is available from any of the Awarding Bodies validating the NVQ. This body will also be able to assist you with titles of useful texts to help you structure the underpinning of knowledge for your in-house candidates, should you choose that route.

IN-HOUSE STAFF DEVELOPMENT

Training can take the form of 'on the job' opportunities supplemented by external courses, events and seminars. Budgets for training will, of course, need to be included at an early stage in the provision for running costs. To supplement your own training work and to incorporate fresh experiences you can explore the training opportunities available from the following:

- the local authority – both education and Early Years Development and Childcare Partnership
- local colleges – these also cover topics such as administration and computer training
- National Children's Bureau – this agency publishes a list of vocational seminars each year
- National Standards – as we have seen elsewhere, the advent of National Standards has made the manager's job if not easier at least more systematic, and this is also the case with training. The Standards include within them an Appendix 1 that gives a selection of organisations offering training as a starting point and a website address where further information and advice may be sought.

TRAINING REQUIREMENTS

There are certain training components that are required by law. These are that:
- 50% of staff must hold recognised qualifications to meet the needs of the Children Act and satisfy the Ofsted inspection
- at least one member of staff must have expertise in special needs and function as the SENCO
- at least one member of staff should hold a Food Handler's Certificate if food is served on the premises
- at least one member of staff should hold a current First Aid Certificate or equivalent issued by the Red Cross or St John Ambulance Brigade. These requirements should be checked with the local inspector.

It is also desirable to have members of staff specifically trained in the following areas:
- managing children's behaviour
- HIV awareness
- equal opportunities
- anti-discriminatory practice
- multicultural curriculum
- keeping children's records
- child protection.

All members of staff also need to have training in the early years curriculum that is provided by individual EYDCPs.

In the nursery

In-service training is an essential part of the on-going work and development of the staff in childcare. Providing good-quality childcare requires considerable skill and abilities. By offering training and learning opportunities, staff are helped to develop their full potential to the benefit of the childcare service they are providing.

See Sample 50 on the CD-Rom.

Continuing Professional Development (CPD)

All professional/vocational staff need to set up a continuing professional development file. A slim file should be obtained and all original qualifications, certificates, records of courses attended and copies of appraisal or other feedback should be included. Documents should be protected and inserted in chronological order, earliest first.

If new staff arrive without a CPD they should be helped to put one together. A typical list of contents might be:

- career profile or overview
- certificate of O Levels or GCSEs from Awarding Body
- certificate of A Levels from Awarding Body
- Vocational Diploma Certificate from CACHE/BTEC/NVQ
- Food Handling Certificate from City & Guilds
- First Aid Certificate from St John
- Induction Completion Pro-forma from another nursery
- Attendance Certificate in Child Protection (from any EYDCP)
- Attendance Certificate in Managing Children's Behaviour (from any EYDCP)
- Attendance Certificate in Foundation Early Years Curriculum (from any EYDCP)
- Staff Appraisal Pro-forma from another nursery
- Attendance Certificate in cases of Attention Deficit Disorder (from any EYDCP)
- NVQ Assessor Award from OCR/CACHE/City & Guilds.

Once signed and authenticated (which means an authority figure has seen the original) photocopies of qualifications might be held in a personal file, with all original certificates secure in the owner's possession. Discourage staff from storing their CPD file in an inaccessible place and ask them to produce it at annual appraisals and Ofsted inspections.

National Vocational Qualifications (NVQs)

NVQ awards were introduced for staff already involved in vocational work – whether full time or part time, waged or unwaged. There is a series of NVQs specifically designed for those working in childcare and education.

A candidate may be assessed for an NVQ without having gained any previous qualifications or undertaken any previous courses or forms of study. However, they will have to show that they have the required underpinning knowledge and understanding of childcare in order to be assessed for the award.

There are no examinations – NVQ candidates are assessed on their performance in the work setting against a set of national occupational standards. Assessment is carried out by qualified assessors from the candidate's work place or by peripatetic assessors who operate from the local NVQ Assessment Centre. There are three levels of NVQ:

- *NVQs in Early Years Care and Education at Level 2*. This NVQ is designed for those staff who work under the supervision of others.
- *NVQs in Early Years Care and Education at Level 3*. This is designed for staff who work without supervision or in supervising others.
  - Each of the qualifications is a combination of core units and optional units. Core units represent work carried out in a wide range of childcare settings. Optional units represent more specialised areas of work – for example, babies or special needs. The standards for these awards are under constant review.
- *NVQ in Early Years Care and Education at Level 4*. This award has three strands: Advanced Practitioner, Management and Quality Assurance.

To achieve an NVQ at any level, a candidate must be assessed as being competent in all of the core units and in all of the optional units chosen (which will reflect the candidate's particular work setting).

NVQs are relevant to the manager and can be used in achieving the following objectives in the work place:

- as a means of staff development, for both qualified and unqualified staff
- as a means of quality upgrading, by focusing on the National Occupational Standard Working With Young Children and their Families (NOSWWYCF)
- as a method of supervision, by assessing the work of colleagues
- as a means of development for qualified staff by becoming an Assessor or Verifier.

Two tables below illustrate various roles in childcare and their relevant awards.

TABLES OF ACCREDITED QUALIFICATION

Vocationally related qualifications: early years education and childcare

Vocationally related qualifications	Awarded by	Job roles
Level 2		
Early Years Care and Education (Progression Award)	C & G	Baby sitter/au pair Crèche assistant Homestart worker
Caring for Children (Foundation Award)	CACHE	Mother's help Nursery assistant Parent/toddler
Childcare and Education (Certificate)	CACHE	group assistant Playgroup assistant
Pre-school Practice (Certificate)	CACHE	Pre-school assistant

continued

Developing Skills for Working with Children and Young People (Intermediate certificate)	NCFE	Toy Library worker
Level 3		
Childare and Education (Diploma)	CACHE	Childminder
		Crèche leader
Childminding Practice (Certificate)	CACHE	Manager level
		Nanny
Early Years Care and Education: Welsh medium (Diploma)	CACHE	Nursery supervisor
		Pre-school leader
Pre-school Practice (Diploma)	CACHE	Playgroup leader
		Professional
Professional Development in Work with Children and Young People	CACHE	Registrations/ Inspection officer
Early Years (BTEC National Certificate)	Edexcel	Supporter
		Toy library leader
Early Years (BTEC National Diploma)	Edexcel	

Occupational qualifications: early years education and children

Occupational qualifications	Awarded by	Job roles
Level 2		
Early years care and education (NVQ)	C & G CACHE Edexcel Open University	Baby sitters/au pair Crèche assistant Homestart worker Mother's help Nursery assistant Parent/toddler group assistant Playgroup assistant Pre-school assistant Toy library worker
Level 3		
Early years care and education (NVQ)	C & G CACHE Edexcel Open University	Childminder Crèche leader Manager level Nanny Nursery supervisor Playgroup leader Pre-school leader Registrations/ Inspection officer Special educational needs supporter Toy library leader

continued

Level 4		
Early years care and education (NVQ)	C & G CACHE	Advanced practitioner Development officer manager: larger/multiple settings Playwork manager

THE NVQ AS A MEANS OF DEVELOPMENT AND QUALITY UPGRADING

NVQs may be used as a helpful framework for developing staff at all levels and for improving the quality of the service.

Unqualified staff (will no longer be able to work in the nursery after 2005)
Staff who, for various reasons, are not qualified but work well with the children will be able to gain recognition for their existing skills and be assessed for additional skills by undertaking the NVQ in Early Years Care and Education. They can start work in the areas where they feel confident and, by careful planning and support, move into the more difficult units. This allows supervision for these candidates/staff members. There is also a Certificate in ChildCare Practice obtainable by accreditation of prior learning for serving staff.

Staff development for qualified staff
Qualified staff can add to their academic achievements by undertaking an Advanced Diploma in Childcare and Education or professional programmes offered in further and higher education establishments – for example, a Foundation Degree in Early Years.

Qualified staff can be encouraged to train as Assessors for NVQ. The training as such is not difficult and staff grow enormously from the process (although assembling documentary evidence to prove their competence can be daunting – the Awarding Bodies are working towards helping staff with this issue).

Assessors are trained under the Employment Occupational Standards Council, which publish and control the assessment standards. They are the industry lead body for training and development, employment and personnel.

The assessor award can be made specifically for childcare by CACHE. The assessor award has excellent development potential and has been the catalyst for much progression since NVQs were first offered in childcare in 1990/91.

A further development at the NVQ Level 4 is Management, which is national and covers all occupations and which has supervisory management units taken from the Management Charter Initiative as well as other vocationally selected areas.

The assessing of both sorts of training has the effect of improving the quality of childcare because familiarity with the National Occupational Standard Working With Young Children and their Families (NOSWWYCF) means that staff are constantly confronted with the details of good practice.

It is common today for small chains or corporate nurseries to become NVQ Assessment Centres in their own right and this has many obvious attractions.

GOOD PRACTICE

A copy of NOSWWYCF should be available for staff to consult whether or not the nursery is involved with NVQs.

The process of supervising staff can be combined with the assessing role and the trust that will then develop around the advice and counselling which follow can only enhance the cohesion and confidence of the team.

The appraisal process

Appraisals are regular meetings between manager and subordinate, providing a non-threatening routine occasion when work standards can be discussed and suggestions for improvement can be jointly decided upon.

Appraisals can either be bottom-up or top-down:

- Bottom-up is from parents to nursery officers, from nursery officers to managers, from managers to daycare inspectors, etc. This system is very popular and widely used in the USA but has never really taken hold in the UK.
- Top-down is from directors to heads of regions to heads of functional units to heads of sections to managers and so to operatives – in our case, nursery staff. This is the system most commonly used in the UK.

Appraisals are designed to assess and improve performance and to suggest training input where appropriate. In some systems again generally in American companies performance scores are kept but these are probably not appropriate for the childcare service.

In some systems one worker is allowed to appraise only two or three others, for example the manager may appraise the heads of areas. These heads would then appraise officers in charge of rooms or sections, who, in turn, would appraise their senior nursery staff and they the juniors, and so forth. This has advantages but could also be hazardous.

THE PURPOSE OF A PERFORMANCE APPRAISAL SYSTEM

Conducting an appraisal

There are a number of possible reasons for introducing performance appraisal into a childcare service organisation. These include:
■ providing feedback on individual staff performance
■ providing staff with a basis for self-evaluation
■ providing a non-threatening routine occasion when work standards are discussed
■ establishing and monitoring objectives and targets
■ reviewing salary, conditions of service and other rewards
■ providing a basis for promotion, dismissal, probation, etc.
■ diagnosing training and career development needs (updating Continuing Professional Development file)
■ maintaining equity in treatment of staff
■ discovering individual (and nursery) potential
■ monitoring the effectiveness of policies and procedures.
Experience of the appraisal process within a large number of organisations suggests that not all these purposes can be achieved within one appraisal scheme, and that any institution has therefore to make careful selection of the key purpose that it wishes the scheme to serve.

In practice it is possible to classify three general types of scheme:
■ those that are related to personnel management needs, e.g. upgrading discipline
■ those that are primarily concerned with improving current and future performance in the childcare service, e.g. curriculum, children's review

- those that are designed to develop the individual and the team, e.g. to uncover training needs, update Continuing Professional Development files.

In the nursery

All appraisal documentation, such as prompt sheets and forms, needs to be considered carefully. Examples of these are provided on the CD-Rom. It will be necessary to adapt these materials to make them suitable for use in a particular nursery. This work might be carried out by the whole staff working group depending on the size of the nursery. In addition to ensuring documentation is suitable for use in a particular nursery, steps should be taken to produce appraisal forms that are consistent with other nursery documents.

See Samples 52–57 on the CD-Rom.

OPEN VERSUS CLOSED QUESTIONS

When conducting an appraisal interview with a member of staff, consider what type of questions you need to ask in order to gather the information required, e.g. whether you should use open questions, closed questions, probing questions, reflective questions and so forth.

Although closed questions are useful for checking specific pieces of information, open questions will usually allow for long informative answers. However, even open questions need to be chosen carefully. Questions that begin with 'why?' may reveal less than those that begin with 'how?' or 'what?'. The first tends to suggest that a justification is required, the others ask for an explanation or description of a process.

For example: avoid	*'Do you think those children are badly behaved?'* (closed) *'How's the curriculum planning group – no difficulty?'* (closed)
Ask	*'What do you think of those children?'* (open) *'Tell me about your plans for the curriculum.'* (open)

Always try to avoid questions that suggest one answer is expected rather than another.

Appraisal interviews

BEFORE THE APPRAISAL INTERVIEW

- Issue self-appraisal forms to staff and arrange the time and location well in advance, and do not allow postponement by either side.
- Decide what information you want to collect from the interview. Make a list of important points to be covered.
- Aim to be systematic; plan to collect all the information about one area

before moving on to another. Try to bear in mind a picture of the complete interview in terms of the information to be collected, rather than in terms of the questions to be asked.

AT THE START OF THE INTERVIEW

- Clearly explain the purpose of the interview and agree an agenda for the meeting that is acceptable to both parties. Fix a closure time, e.g. 'complete before the children's lunch/sleep time'.
- Make the staff member to be appraised feel comfortable and able to talk freely. Remember that an effective appraisal is a two-way discussion, and you need to address the issues raised by the staff member as well as deal with your own or the nursery's agenda.

DURING THE INTERVIEW

- Focus on the responsibilities and goals of the appraisee rather than on their character traits.
- Make notes because you are unlikely to remember enough detail to do so afterwards, particularly if you are conducting a number of appraisal interviews; however, avoid making notes in an officious way.
- Do not try to do things in the interview that are best done at another time and in a different way, e.g. give out work for the following week or discuss a key child.
- Where appropriate, explore the answer that the staff member gives you. Do not assume that because he or she has talked after you asked a question, they gave you the information you wanted.
- Deal constructively with disagreement; if both of you are discussing the important issues in performance there will often be a legitimate difference of view about what should be done. A good appraisal is an opportunity for tackling such disagreements in a constructive way.
- Deal constructively with apathy. If the staff member appears apathetic about the process (e.g. 'What's the point?') then deal with the issue of apathy; if you do not do so, the interview will be a waste of time. You might then have to arrange another appointment.
- Do not be aggressive or ask trick questions.
- Avoid showing excessive approval, disapproval, scepticism or even surprise.
- Ask one question at a time. Multiple questions are confusing for everyone (especially avoid multiple questions that confuse information with judgements: e.g. 'What outings have you arranged for your group, or don't you get on with them well enough to ask parents?').
- Once you have asked a question, wait for an answer; short silences are not necessarily a bad thing and may get a nervous person talking.
- Let the colleague finish what he or she is saying without interruption.

- Listen carefully (see the Activity on developing active listening skills in Chapter 8) and concentrate on what the staff member is saying; do not talk unnecessarily yourself.

AFTER THE INTERVIEW

- Ensure that agreements made in the appraisal are acted upon and that agreed deadlines are met.
- Both parties should sign and date a record for (1) the Continuing Professional Development file and (2) inspection.

BENEFITS OF APPRAISAL

The benefits of appraisal are:
- performance improvement
- identification of training needs and updating Continuing Professional Development file
- facilitation of decision-making
- monitoring the health of the organisation
- increased motivation and productivity.

Appraisal will help the manager to:
- increase staff performance
- improve motivation and commitment
- keep staff well informed
- have more insight and better relationships
- reduce the likelihood of unforeseen difficulties
- keep in touch with issues in the nursery.

Activity
Study the above list of benefits of introducing an appraisal system. Are there any more that you can think of? Make your own list.

DIFFICULTIES OF APPRAISAL

Listed below are some of the main problems nurseries have encountered when implementing appraisal systems for the first time.
- Employees fear unfair or subjective judgements and therefore find the process threatening.
- If the appraisal is badly conducted, it is very demotivating.
- Management reluctance to tackle performance problems and conduct reviews often has to be overcome.
- Inadequate training in the concept and processes, often the result of undue haste, causes systems to fail.
- Failure to see performance review management as a continuing process limits its benefits.

- Unnecessarily complicated systems make them unattractive to nursery staff.
- Lack of top management commitment to the process, as well as the idea, limits credibility.
- Trying to introduce systems that are alien to the culture raises the risk of rejection.
- Trying to introduce systems faster than the existing culture can absorb them results in patchy implementation.
- Failure to communicate the new values prevents staff understanding the benefits.

Activity
Study the above list of difficulties of introducing an appraisal system. Are there any more that you can think of? Make your own list.

In the nursery
It is essential that staff are made familiar with the aims of the appraisal system and with the procedures involved. The documents should be taken to the staff meeting and discussed fully before any attempt is made to put the system in place.

See Samples 52–57 on the CD-Rom.

Self-appraisal

Self-appraisal has come to be seen both as an important ingredient in any formal appraisal scheme and as valuable for any nursery worker or teacher. Within an appraisal scheme, self-reflective appraisal can occur at a number of points.

- Self-appraisal may be a useful form of preparation for an appraisee before an initial meeting. At this point, self-appraisal can help to clarify possible areas to put forward for development during the rest of the appraisal process.
- Self-appraisal can also be useful immediately before the appraisal interview. Placed at this point in the process, it can help the appraisee to come to the interview prepared and with his or her own thoughts in order.
- Self-appraisal can also be encouraged by the way in which the different components of the appraisal process are arranged. For example, child observation targeted towards agreed areas and followed by feedback and discussion will encourage reflection and self-appraisal. Self-appraisal can therefore contribute successfully at several points during the appraisal process.

Within a formal appraisal scheme, self-appraisal can be approached in various ways, as follows:

- putting aside some time for quiet, unstructured reflection
- free writing, i.e. writing about your job and how you feel it is going in an unstructured way
- writing about your job with reference to a job description or list of key tasks
- writing about your job and how you feel it is going, with the help of a few prompting questions
- using a self-rating prompt sheet, where you are asked to rate your performance in various aspects of your work according to a numerical or verbal scale (see Sample 57 on the CD-Rom)
- listing various tasks, for which you are responsible, and ranking them in order of the success you feel you have achieved in them
- completing prompting sentences that help you to explore the various aspects of your work
- evaluating your performance in the light of previously agreed objectives and criteria of success.

In essence, all these approaches are designed to facilitate personal reflection. The best approach is a matter of individual taste, though the different approaches do tend to vary in their emphasis.

Self-appraisal should not only be seen as part of the appraisal process. It is also, in a more or less informal way, a regular feature of nursery work. It is a rare childcare worker who does not reflect upon how an activity went or on what came out of a meeting. Indeed, one aim of a formal appraisal scheme might well be to encourage this form of on-going reflection, perhaps making it more targeted and constructive. However, whether self-appraisal is formal or informal, certain difficulties can occur.

Look out for the following problems in carrying out self-appraisal.

- *The 'blind spot':* people can be unaware of a particular strength or weakness or may simply prefer to ignore it. Structured appraisal prompt lists may help staff to focus on all aspects of their job, and make it more difficult to overlook particular areas.
- *Being too self-critical:* some people, especially those with an internal locus of control, are excessively hard on themselves, minimising successes and agonising over difficulties. In these cases, self-appraisal could become an exercise in self-criticism and prove an unsettling experience.
- *Confidentiality:* the question arises as to whether comments recorded during self-appraisal should be shared directly with the appraiser.

CASE STUDY

The potential dangers of self-appraisal are outweighed by the many benefits of self-appraisal, as the following nursery workers tell us:

'The whole process wouldn't have been much good without it [self-appraisal].'

'I think that development has to come from self-analysis. Once you recognise what you need to do, you're more likely to go ahead and do it.'

In the nursery
Self-appraisal can:
- bring about individual commitment to change
- ensure that appraisal is a two-way process
- ensure that the appraisee clarifies his or her thoughts before meeting the appraiser and thus knows what he or she wants from the process
- bring about a greater feeling of professionalism, for at the heart of professionalism is the concept of self-monitoring
- encourage the habit of on-going reflection, carried out in a constructive spirit and on the basis of a desire to celebrate success and to work on improvements.

See Samples 52–57 on the CD-Rom.

KEYS TO GOOD PRACTICE
- On-going staff development is an essential part of nursery life. Ensure a regular development programme is in place. Include (1) in-house items for all staff (e.g. curriculum, procedures) and (2) external input (e.g. from colleges, local Early Years Development and Childcare Partnership, NCB, Open University, Open College).
- A copy of NOSWWYCF should be available in the nursery, whether the centre is involved in NVQs or not.
- Staff appraisal should be adopted as an invaluable technique for quality supervision.
- Self-appraisal should be viewed as a valuable tool for a childcare worker.
- All staff should keep a living Continuing Professional Development file.

PART IV

STRATEGIES FOR MANAGING THE CURRICULUM IN EARLY YEARS PROVISION

What this chapter covers:
- what is a curriculum?
- historical influences on the early years curriculum
- research and developments
- the manager's role in curriculum delivery
- the foundation stage or early years curriculum
- the framework for practitioners with babies
- management strategies for planning the curriculum
- the role of the manager and the Qualification and Curriculum Authority (QCA).

This chapter is about managing the curriculum – with a heavy emphasis on managing. Strategies to bring in the curriculum were, until recently, a neglected area and it is this aspect of the manager's role that we will concentrate on in this chapter.

What exactly do we mean by 'curriculum'?

It is useful to be clear about what the term 'curriculum' actually means as it is one that frightens some early years carers. In its broadest sense, curriculum is a total learning package constructed deliberately to enhance the development and facilitate the learning of an individual or a group of individuals. For example, the curriculum of a module in a childcare course has three main components. There is also a value base to these components. In childcare this would be a strong ethical value base. (In other vocational areas the value base may more appropriately be commercial.) All of the above – together with the syllabus, the physical attendance, the methods used and the 'own time' activities such as reading, homework and other preparation – will be documented and will collectively form the *curriculum*.

HIDDEN CURRICULUM

In addition to what is documented publicly there is always a 'hidden curriculum', i.e. one that is not deliberately constructed or planned and that is not written down but which happens anyway. In the example on page 146

EXAMPLE OF A CURRICULUM OF A MODULE

1. Syllabus of the module	The list of the areas of knowledge the students will be taught.	■ Child development, 0–8 years. ■ Social and psychology factors affecting this development. ■ Educational philosophy of Frobel, Steiner and Montessori. ■ Reading list to reflect above.
2. Structure of the module	The shape or pattern of attendance.	■ Day Release ■ Short Full-Time ■ Evening Course ■ Distance Learning
3. Methodology for the module	How the learning is going to be delivered using the activities of the teacher and of the students.	■ Lectures/Expositions ■ Seminar Groups/Discussion Groups ■ Workshops/Films/Group Tasks ■ Group Activities/Tutorials/Projects ■ Visits and Exhibition of Work

(Note: Methodology is not only what teachers do, but also what students do.)

the hidden curriculum might be making new friends, learning how groups work and learning how you function in a new group situation.

APPLICATION TO THE NURSERY

When applying this model to early years it will be obvious that the methodology, i.e. the children's and adult's activities, will be by far the largest part of the whole curriculum.

Activity

Think of a course you have attended recently and consider which area of the curriculum contributed most to you in your development as a whole person. Was it:

- the knowledge you gained
- the activities you undertook
- the group discussion or activities

or was it:

- the chats over coffee
- the new friends you made
- the laughs you had.

Was this part of the set curriculum or the hidden curriculum?

We all learn most when we are enjoying the activity in which we are engaged. Play is the activity that children enjoy most and from which they learn most. They learn from:

- all the activities and experiences they devise themselves
- all the materials and resources provided by adults
- all they see and hear around them
- the language they use with their peers
- the language adults use with them.

Play – as we all know and as mentioned below – is a child's 'work'; it is extremely serious, totally absorbing and very necessary. It creates opportunities for the children to:

- form their first peer group
- make discoveries about themselves and the world in which they live, in their own time and at their own pace
- organise and re-organise and support their experiences
- consolidate their learning
- collect and express their thoughts
- develop language and communication systems
- develop concentration and perseverance
- develop physical, social, emotional and intellectual skills through first-hand experiences.

The expertise needed in planning an early years curriculum is the ability to manage a child's 'play' activities in such a way that they will lead to all of the

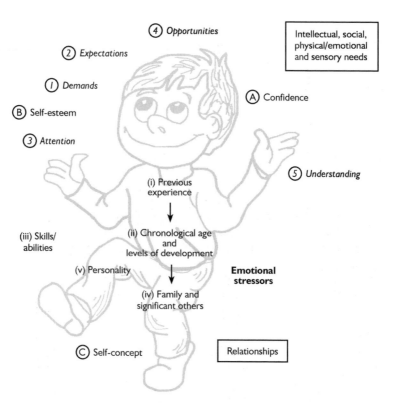

4 *Opportunities*

2 *Expectations*

Intellectual, social, physical/emotional and sensory needs

1 *Demands*

B *Self-esteem*

A *Confidence*

3 *Attention*

5 *Understanding*

(i) Previous experience

↓

(iii) Skills/ abilities

(ii) Chronological age and levels of development

(v) Personality

Emotional stressors

(iv) Family and significant others

C *Self-concept*

Relationships

An interactive view of behaviour: everything affects everything else

above and will lay a sound foundation for future, more structured learning. This will contribute to a confident young person progressing to a school environment.

The syllabus part of the curriculum for the 3 to 5s will not differ much from that of older children. Only the methods and activities will vary with the children's age – the discipline areas are exactly the same. So, even for the very young children the curriculum will have a syllabus that includes the items on Sample 34 on the CD-Rom (this list is not intended to be fully comprehensive).

If all the materials mentioned in delivering the early years programme were assembled and set out safely, they would produce the ideal environment for delivering the curriculum.

Children have a natural desire to learn and it is through playing with real objects that they begin to make sense of their world. The importance of play should always be respected in the devising of the nursery curriculum.

Activity

Make a list of all the equipment you might put together to provide one aspect of the foundation curriculum, e.g. physical development.

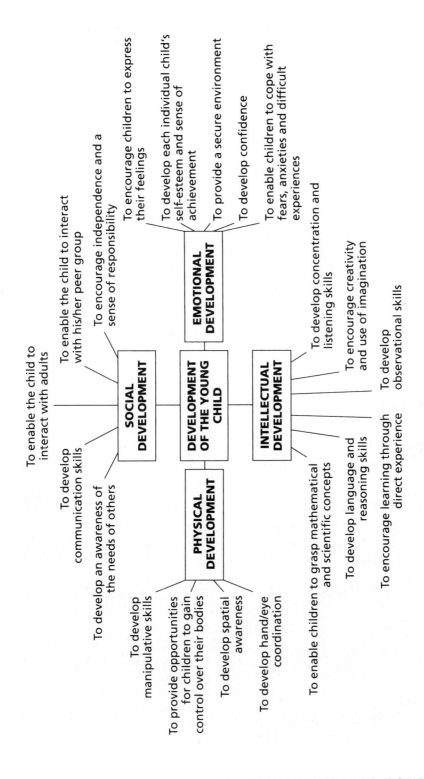

Aims of nursery education

It is the manager's responsibility to ensure that the rich environment required to foster the child's development is in place in the nursery. Remember that in providing a syllabus for very young children, attention must be paid to all aspects of the child, i.e.

PHYSICAL DEVELOPMENT
INTELLECTUAL DEVELOPMENT
EMOTIONAL DEVELOPMENT
SOCIAL DEVELOPMENT

As we have noted, it is impossible to separate one aspect of a child's development from another but this old, much-favoured mnemonic provides a model to structure reflection during the planning process.

GOOD PRACTICE

Special reference must be made to language. Language acquisition underpins all aspects of any early years programme. Supported children will spontaneously provide a constant commentary to their activities. Much of a professional worker's skill is in extending this spontaneous talk, facilitating good language development. *Every adult* interacting with a child is a *teacher of language* – a sombre thought.

Historical influences on the early years curriculum

As already noted, it is the manager's responsibility to plan, implement and review the curriculum. However, the choice or control of the philosophy underpinning the curriculum on offer will depend very much on the conditions in which the nursery is run, who owns it, who governs it and so forth.

In UK mainstream nursery school education it is usual to find a curriculum based on the teachings of Froebel (1782–1852), a German early years pioneer who advocated an informal structure, and who first noticed that 'Play is a child's work'.

Froebel's approach provided a fertile backdrop for those who followed, who adopted and adapted his teachings – Margaret McMillan and Susan Issacs being perhaps the most famous. It is on the work of these educators that the mainstream early years curriculum is now based. The informal structure lends itself well to the changing needs of our educational system.

Froebel allowed great flexibility, and the children's active planning, doing and reviewing advocated by the Highscope researchers in America was readily compatible with the public sector schools curriculum and has become widely used since it was first introduced to the UK.

It is interesting to note that both Maria Montessori and Rudolf Steiner in their times developed their educational 'methods' and curriculum for just such children. Both these educationalists devised different but formally structured closed methods of education. In their pure form these have survived only in the private sector – at least in the UK, but, like Froebel, they both have training systems bearing their name.

Montessori saw children as existing in a separate miniature world and did not advocate group interaction until the child arrived at the notion independently. Neither did she advocate much adult contribution – not even from the 'directresses' whom she trained in her systems and who set up the all-important environment in which the children were to develop.

The manager employed in either a Montessori or a Rudolf Steiner School will already have a method and a curriculum structure to guide their planning. The manager's involvement will therefore be as a guide and advisor ensuring that the presentation of the work is in sympathy with the needs of modern parents and children. Montessori herself would have been most reluctant to modify her approach, whatever the 1989 Act demanded in respect to parents. Steiner, on the other hand, believed that parents were natural educators and would have approved of recent development.

Managers in charge of private day-care settings may have the most powerful voice in respect of the curriculum and elect for the 'eclectic' approach – incorporating the simplicity of the Montessori environment and equipment with the community spirit of Steiner, the flexibility of Froebel, and the active planning, doing and reviewing of Highscope.

The approach used will be dependent on the ages of the children and the level of their development. All the pioneers agree that the child's development is precious in its own right – Froebel orders us that 'at every stage, be that stage'. The child's development should not be accelerated but should be enjoyed with the child for its value in the totality of their life experiences.

Whichever early years theorist is favoured, the curriculum's aims will still adhere to the *ten common principles*, which are as follows.

1. Childhood is a valid point of life and not merely a preparation for adulthood.
2. The whole child is important – physical, intellectual, emotional, social and spiritual.
3. Learning is not compartmentalised – everything is connected.
4. Intrinsic motivation resulting in self-directed activity is valued.
5. Self-discipline is emphasised.
6. There are specially receptive stages of development when periods of learning occur.
7. What the child can – as opposed to cannot – do is the starting point in their education.
8. All children have an inner life, which emerges under favourable conditions.
9. The people, both adults and children, with whom the child interacts are of central importance.
10. The child's education is seen as an interaction between the child and

the environment, including in particular other people and knowledge itself.

Tina Bruce in *Early Childhood Education* (1987) offers a most interesting résumé of these principles and an analysis of how each is supported by the work of all three pioneers.

As has been noted throughout the text there was a great dearth of management research in the early years context. This is less true in respect to the curriculum.

Research and developments

EFFECTIVE PROVISION OF PRE-SCHOOL EDUCATION (EPPE)

This longitudinal study involving 3,000 children between the ages of 3 and 7 years was set up in 1997. Its aims were as follows.

- To produce a detailed description of the 'career paths' of a large sample of children and their families between entry into pre-school education and completion (or near completion) of Key Stage 1.
- To compare and contrast the developmental progress of 3,000+ children from a wide range of social and cultural background who have differing pre-school experiences, including early entry to Reception from home.
- To separate out the effects of pre-school experience from the effects of education in the period between Reception and Year 2.
- To establish whether some pre-school centres are more effective than others in promoting children's cognitive and social/emotional development during the pre-school years (ages 3–5) and the beginning of primary education (5–7 years).
- To discover the individual characteristics (structural and process) of pre-school education in those centres found to be most effective.
- To investigate differences in the process of different groups of children, e.g. second language learners of English, children from disadvantaged backgrounds and both genders.
- To investigate the medium-term effects of pre-school education on educational performance at Key Stage 1 in a way which will allow the possibility of longitudinal follow-up at later ages to establish long-term effects, if any.
- To relate the use of pre-school provision to parental labour market participation.

Six local authorities and six main types of provision (i.e. playgroups, day and private nurseries, nursery school, nursery classes, and centres combining care and education) were involved. The samples were chosen at random across the authorities provision, in a total of 141 centres.

A further sample of 200 children not attending any pre-school provision were recruited as a control group. In March 2003 the project reported their findings, which in brief are as follows.

Impact of attending a pre-school centre

1. Pre-school experience, compared to none, enhances children's development.
2. The duration of attendance is important, with an earlier start being related to better intellectual development and improved independence, concentration and sociability.
3. Full-time attendance led to no better gains for children than part-time provision.
4. Disadvantaged children in particular can benefit significantly from good-quality pre-school experiences, especially if they attend centres that cater for a mixture of children from different social backgrounds.

The quality and practices in pre-school centres

5. The quality of pre-school centres is directly related to better intellectual/cognitive and social-behavioural development in children.
6. Good quality can be found across all types of early years settings. However, quality was higher overall in integrated settings, nursery schools and nursery classes.
7. Settings that have staff with higher qualifications, especially with a good proportion of trained teachers on the staff, show higher quality and their children make more progress.
8. Where settings view educational and social development as complementary and equal in importance, children make better all-round progress.
9. Effective pedagogy includes interaction traditionally associated with the term 'teaching', the provision of instructive learning environments and 'sustained shared thinking' to extend children's learning.

Type of pre-school

10. There are significant differences between individual pre-school settings in their impact on children. Some settings are more effective than others in promoting positive child outcomes.
11. Children tend to make better intellectual progress in fully integrated centres and nursery schools.

The quality of home learning

12. The quality of the learning environment of the home (where the parents are actively engaged in activities with children) promoted intellectual and social development in all children. Although parents' social class and levels of education were related to child outcomes the quality of the home-learning environment was more important. The home-learning environment is only moderately associated with social class. What parents do is more important than who they are.

These findings are of great importance to managers, with particular reference to integrating education and care (11), and placing great value on parental involvement (12) – thus suggesting these should be reflected in the environment the manager creates. Finding No. 7 should also be borne in mind during recruitment and staff development.

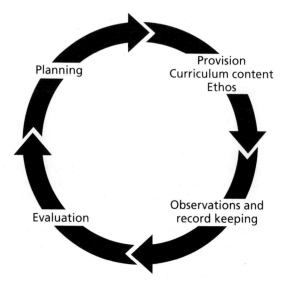

It is the manager's job to be aware of on-going research and to ensure that the children benefit from her expertise.

The manager's role in curriculum delivery

The role of the manager in an early years setting in relation to the curriculum is to:
- ensure that the children are given a quality service, which includes the early curriculum – the foundation stage
- consult and respect the wishes of the parents/carers, who are rightly becoming more demanding in terms of appropriate curriculum input
- support and supervise the staff who give this service and deliver the curriculum
- provide adequate resources to enable the curriculum to function well
- set up a rich and stimulating environment in which the aims and principles of early childhood education can be delivered hold records of same for use at Ofsted inspections.

It is the manager's role to plan, implement and evaluate the planning process, working closely with the nursery team.

The foundation stage or early years curriculum

In arranging the curriculum, staff will expect to provide for the development of the whole child for each individual child and will expect to maximise the child's potential in accordance with the underlying principles of early years education.

PRINCIPLES FOR EARLY YEARS EDUCATION

(Taken from the Department for Education and Skills with QCA 2000 publication *Curriculum Guidance for the Foundation Stage*.)

These principles are drawn from, and are evident in, good and effective practice in early years settings.

- Effective education requires both a relevant curriculum and practitioners who understand and are able to implement the curriculum requirements.
- Effective education requires practitioners who understand that children develop rapidly during the early years – physically, intellectually, emotionally and socially. Children are entitled to provision that supports and extends knowledge, skills, understanding and confidence, and helps them to overcome any disadvantage.
- Practitioners should ensure that all children feel included, secure and valued. They must build positive relationships with parents in order to work effectively with them and their children.
- Early years experience should build on what children already know and can do. It should also encourage a positive attitude and disposition to learn and aim to prevent early failure.
- No child should be excluded or disadvantaged because of ethnicity, culture, religion, home language, family background, special educational needs, disability, gender or ability.
- Parents and practitioners should work together in an atmosphere of mutual respect within which children can have security and confidence.
- To be effective, an early years curriculum should be carefully structured. In that structure, there should be three strands:
  - provision for the different starting points from which children develop their learning, building on what they already do
  - relevant and appropriate content that matches the different levels of young children's needs
  - planned and purposeful activity that provides opportunities for teaching and learning, both indoors and outdoors.
- There should be opportunities for children to engage in activities planned by adults and also those that they plan or initiate themselves. Children do not make a distinction between 'play' and 'work' and neither should practitioners. Children need time to become engrossed, work in depth and complete activities.
- Practitioners must be able to observe and respond appropriately to children, informed by a knowledge of how children develop and learn and a clear understanding of possible next steps in their development and learning.
- Well-planned, purposeful activity and appropriate intervention by practi-

tioners will engage children in the learning process and help them make progress in their learning.

- For children to have rich and stimulating experiences, the learning environment should be well planned and well organised. It provides the structure for teaching within which children explore, experiment, plan and make decisions for themselves, thus enabling them to learn, develop and make good progress.
- Above all, effective learning and development for young children requires high-quality care and education by practitioners.

These principles are the basis on which every part of this guidance has been developed, and are reflected throughout.

The Framework for practitioners with babies

A Framework for practitioners with babies from birth to three years is also available for support and guidance.

THE PURPOSE OF THE FRAMEWORK

The purpose of the Framework is to provide support, information, guidance and challenge for all those with responsibility for the care and education of babies and children from birth to three years. The Framework:

- values and celebrates babies and children
- recognises their individuality, efforts and achievements
- recognises that all children have from birth a need to develop, learning through interaction with people and exploration of the world around them. For some people, this development may be at risk because of difficulties with communication and interaction, cognition and learning, behavioural, emotional and social development or sensory and physical development
- recognises the 'holistic' nature of development and learning, and acknowledges, values and supports the adults that work with babies and young children
- provides opportunities for reflection on practice
- informs and develops practice, while acknowledging that working with babies and children is a complex, challenging and demanding task and that often there are no easy answers.

THE FRAMEWORK IN CONTEXT

It is important that the Framework is considered within the context of the *National Standards for Under Eights Daycare and Childminding* (DfES, 2001) together with the *Curriculum Guidance for the Foundation Stage* (DfES/QCA, 2000).

WHO IS THE FRAMEWORK FOR?

This Framework is for all those who work with and care for children aged birth to three, including those children with SEN and/or disability. It is intended to be used flexibly by practitioners, individually and in groups.

PRINCIPLES THAT UNDERPIN THE FRAMEWORK

- Parents and families are central to the well-being of the child.
- Relationships with other people (both adults and children) are of crucial importance in a child's life.
- A relationship with a key person at home and in the setting is essential to young children's well-being.
- Babies and young children are social beings; they are competent learners from birth.
- Learning is a shared process and children learn most effectively when, with the support of a knowledgeable and trusted adult, they are actively involved and interested.
- Caring adults count more than resources and equipment.
- Schedules and routines must flow with the child's needs.
- Children learn when they are given appropriate responsibility, allowed to make errors, decisions and choices, and respected as autonomous and competent learners.
- Children learn by doing rather than by being told.
- Young children are vulnerable. They learn to be independent by having someone they can depend upon.

HOW THE FRAMEWORK IS ORGANISED

The Framework takes as its focus the child and steers away from subjects, specific areas of experience and distinct curriculum headings. It identifies four 'Aspects', which celebrate the skill and competence of babies and young children and highlight interrelationships between growth, learning, development and the environment in which they are cared for and educated.

These four Aspects are:
- a strong child
- a skilful communicator
- a competent learner
- a healthy child.

The Framework offers both theoretical and practical notions on the development of babies.

Management strategies for planning the curriculum

As with policies and procedures, it is very important that all the childcare staff participate in developing and writing the curriculum. This should include students and volunteers (where appropriate).

This is important so that:

- everyone will have a sense of ownership of the curriculum and will deliver it with enthusiasm
- team work is fostered in this area, as in others, and no one is excluded
- there is a consistent approach to the work and also towards individual children, including SEN children
- curriculum planning becomes an integral part of staff development
- the children benefit from all the available creativity of the staff.

The member of staff who has attended training or who has the most appropriate background and skills should be given responsibility for organising the curriculum planning. This need not be the manager – in many ways results will be more controllable if someone else (a curriculum co-ordinator) undertakes this task.

However, as the most experienced and senior member of staff, the manager should attend and contribute fully to all curriculum meetings to signal the high profile given to the children's learning within the centre. If the manager holds on to this work the planning process can so easily be deferred in the midst of the urgency of the hundred other daily tasks. When another professional holds curriculum as a special responsibility – with a reporting system – the work will happen without the manager needing to initiate it every time and the children will benefit accordingly. The reporting system is vital – as mentioned earlier, it is important to delegate not dump.

GOOD PRACTICE

This area is particularly appropriate for job enhancement – see also Chapter 5 on staff motivation.

Delegating curriculum planning

TASKS OF THE CURRICULUM CO-ORDINATOR

It is this curriculum co-ordinator's job to convene the planning meetings and a *bare minimum* for frequency of these is one main planning meeting each term. At this meeting the term's work can be planned and a series of smaller meetings can be arranged for the work to progress.

Even if the nursery is open for the whole year, the curriculum should still follow the traditional academic terms. It makes an excellent contrast for the children if a 'special' programme is written for the long academic break. This programme can be more orientated to small frequent outings and other seasonal activities.

There are three main reasons for the practice of keeping the academic terms for purposes of curriculum planning:

■ to pace and structure the work
■ to minimise disruption for children's holidays
■ to prepare the children for school
■ to facilitate progression.

The *annual planning cycle* has seven phases and will look something like this:

1. September to October   Autumn Curriculum
2. October to December   Winter Curriculum
3. January to February   Winter Curriculum
4. February to March   Spring Curriculum
5. March to May   Spring Curriculum
6. May to July   Summer Curriculum
7. July to September   Special Programme

Activity

In a group, examine the annual planning cycle and, thinking of the fun the children might have, suggest themes for each term or half-term. Be as frivolous as you like!

Care should be taken to avoid exact repetition year after year because:

■ the long-term staff will become stale
■ new team members will not be making their full contribution to the work; they will feel excluded and their creativity will be wasted
■ the resources will lack freshness
■ the older children will become bored even if they do not consciously 'remember' participating in last year's programme.

However, a certain similarity from one year to the next is unavoidable, and even welcome, as children relate well to the familiar. Obviously, the religious festivals also recur and must be included each year.

CHOOSING A THEME FOR THE EARLY YEARS FOUNDATION CURRICULUM

A theme can be identified for each block, whether it be a whole or a half term. Themes can range from a major project to a small interest table.

A major project can involve all classes of a nursery or small groups, each working on a different related topic. It may involve all members of staff and cover all areas of the curriculum.

An isolated project may be relevant to a particular group, and not related to the general theme for the term.

A spontaneous interest table may focus on a topical issue that arises within the group.

GOOD PRACTICE

A calendar of religious festivals is readily available and is an invaluable resource in the planning process and as part of the multi-cultural display.

It is a very good practice to be non-selective in recognition and celebration of religious festivals whichever culture predominates in the nursery. All our children are growing up in a multi-cultural society, and the earlier they develop mutual knowledge of each other, the earlier they will develop mutual trust and respect.

CASE STUDY

'As part of an inspection team I visited a quite prestigious nursery one early December, I found the staff energetically putting up Christmas decorations. I complimented the manager on how pretty they looked and on how hard the staff were working. I followed this by asking "Do you celebrate other festivals in the centre? "Oh yes, Easter" she replied.'

Before the main planning meeting the curriculum co-ordinator should:

- notify staff and prepare in advance a structure for the work, e.g. six- or twelve-week programmes, half term, or one term. Half terms allow flexibility and easy of movement of progressing children (and possibly also staff). See Samples 35, 36, 37 and 38
- ask that they give some thought to the task and bring curriculum ideas with them because everyone will benefit from time spent thinking through aims and objectives
- give the start and finish times of the meeting and adhere to these.

RESOURCES FOR USE AT THE PLANNING MEETING

- A copy of the DfeS/QCA 2000, *Curriculum Guidance on the Foundation Stage*, to stimulate ideas and act as a reminder of the children's learning goals and of the stepping stones.

- Other resource books and professional journals, to stimulate ideas and confirm standards, e.g. *Nursery World*.
- Large sheets of paper/flipcharts, and a selection of writing equipment.
- Other resource materials, e.g. religious festivals calendar, details of planned events in the community, such as the local library.
- Copies of individual plans of the SENCO.
- A proforma for recording a model curriculum embedding the ELG (see Samples 31 and 35).

By the end of the meeting there should be:

1. A theme selected which must be attractive to the adult and potentially attractive to the children. It must be offered at a suitable intellectual level for the group. These could be:
   - seasonal
   - topical, e.g. something that will be covered in the media such as the Olympic Games
   - linked to a particular child, or relevant to the group at that time
   - linked to some object or collection or hobby
   - related to a specific area of the curriculum
   - based specifically on one or more of the senses
   - designed to provide imaginative play stimulus
   - designed to encourage self-awareness or awareness of others
   - selected to introduce an aspect of the child's wider environment and community.
2. A firm commitment from colleagues to contribute themselves and the resources to the work.
3. A programme of smaller meetings to work out details of visits and outings and so forth.
4. A date when the final programme will appear.

The curriculum co-ordinator now:
- starts collecting resources
- involves children in the planning and preparation
- involves parents
- plans to involve the wide environment and community, e.g. by visits and bringing visitors in who have a 'role' in the plan
- plans for 'hands-on' and imaginative play experiences for the children
- is prepared to be flexible as the planning proceeds.

WHY DO WE USE PROJECTS AND THEMES?

- With well-thought out objectives, children will grow in physical, intellectual, emotional and social development.
- Opportunities exist to extend language, general knowledge and understanding, through familiar topics, and to introduce the wider environment and community.

- With thoughtful planning all six areas of the Foundation curriculum can be incorporated.
- Children can be encouraged to develop sensory awareness using all five senses.
- Children can be involved at all stages; then they acquire new concepts, and are curious to find out more.
- The eye-catching displays produced will attract children and parents, and will hold their interest.
- Parents can be invited and encouraged to be involved.
- Particular themes can be of value or special interest to individual children giving them affirmation.
- A theme provides a focus and encourages co-operation from the whole team.
- Themes are fun, with opportunities in all categories of play and for all levels of players.

In the nursery
One method of writing up the plan is to produce a spider diagram. Sample 32 illustrates a seven-week programme using Transport as the theme, chosen because of the interest of one group of children in the nursery concerned.
See Sample 32 on the CD-Rom.

Activity
With a partner, chose a topic using the system above and brainstorm a programme for a group of children of a specified age. If you are ambitious, you could go on to design the curriculum for the school.

GOOD PRACTICE

Where it is at all possible, the work of planning the curriculum should be done in nursery time. Where this is not possible, some recognition should be made of staff attendance out of hours.
Either:
(a) it should be made clear on the appointment of staff that some evening attendance is expected, e.g. for parents' evenings, planning meetings and social events
(b) time off in lieu may be given to staff at a time convenient to the nursery, if finances allow
(c) if it is more appropriate and possible, overtime can be paid.
This is a difficult and sensitive issue. Whatever management policy is adopted, time for planning meetings must be made. The curriculum should never be imposed on the staff. Where job descriptions and circumstances permit, option (a) above is by far the best solution.

It is very poor practice and quite unacceptable to offer the children unplanned or inadequately planned work. Their development will undoubtedly suffer and learning opportunities will be lost forever. There will also be a great loss of morale among the staff and missed opportunities for team building.

The role of the manager and the Qualification and Curriculum Authority (QCA)

In Autumn 1995 the Schools Council Assessment Authority produced the first discussion document offering guidance to providers of Desirable Outcomes for Children's Learning to be achieved by the time they entered school. The SCAA claims that what they offered was not strictly a curriculum (since that was the role of the provider) but they suggested educational activities likely to lead to the 'desirable outcome'.

SCAA was then superseded by Qualification and Curriculum Authority, an arm of the Department for Education and Employment, and in 2001 the Curriculum Guidance for the Foundation Stage and the six Early Learning Goals appeared, replacing but closely resembling the 'desirable outcomes'.

- personal, social and emotional development
- communication, language and literacy
- mathematical development
- knowledge and understanding of the world
- physical development
- creative development.

Dfee and QCA have produced excellent publications to help practitioners deliver this curriculum and training is offered by every EYDCP on a regular basis.

For children able to go beyond the early learning goals QCA suggests it is appropriate to provide the opportunities as already planned and published for Key Stage 1 programmes of the National Curriculum.

Children making slower progress for whatever reason will need carefully differentiated learning opportunities and regular and frequent monitoring.

PARENTAL INVOLVEMENT IN THE CURRICULUM

There are many ways to involve parents, seek their advice and elicit their opinion on the curriculum and their own child's particular needs, and to use any talents or skills they want to share

Open evenings
It is good practice to explain the curriculum to parents. Do not hesitate to use the names of academic subjects as parents often cannot identify early maths, science or literacy in the children's work and play.

Display
The curriculum plan should be on show in the nursery and each work area

should be labelled with some explanation at adult height (see Sample 33 on the CD-Rom).

Personal involvement
Many parents will be happy to come into the nursery and contribute from their own expertise and culture.

CASE STUDY

'A particularly talented nursery professional I know had a vicar's child in her nursery and on occasions when the nursery celebrated a "wedding" this parent would attend appropriately dressed and 'officiate' at the ceremony.

This was a truly wonderful experience for the children. They had science with the cake-making, maths in the table-laying and guest counting, language in the stories and rhymes on the subject, creativity in the music, in the invitations and decorations, all the personal and social development anyone could ask for in the dressing up and role playing involved from uncles to brides and grannies. They also had the vicar's delighted interest and affirmation of their work.

This same teacher invited parents to cook foods from different countries and teach children in small groups in the process. This was during a term when the theme was "Foods".'

Children's work
The children's work should be sent home in protective packets and discussed with the parents. Their work should be mounted and displayed on the walls. Written explanation should be attached where needed, particularly verbatim quotations from the children themselves.

Children's records
Open records are most suitable for the children's records. These should be completed by their keyworker and parents kept informed on their progress.

Shared homework
There are several ways to involve the parents in work with the children at home. Many of these methods were developed in the 1990s for infant school but adapt readily for the younger child.

One very creative example of this is IMPACT MATHS:
Interactive
Maths for
Parents
And
Children and
Teachers.

This system is one in which the child takes home enough information to 'teach' the parent some aspect of maths from that day's work. The parent and child undertake the exercise together and complete the written part of the work; this is then returned to school for the teacher to mark. Similar schemes can be devised for other subjects depending on the local conditions.

In the nursery

Reading together for homework is always a good idea. Parents can be asked to complete a feedback sheet. Nursery books on the selected theme can be 'borrowed' to take home (in plastic envelopes) and returned after reading, e.g. over a weekend.

   See Sample 39 on the CD-Rom.

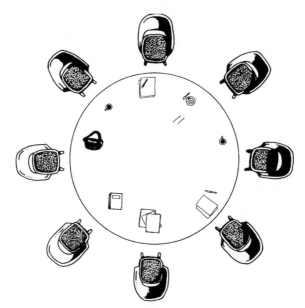

Set up for a curriculum team meeting

Evaluation

Managers should constantly reassess the curriculum provision and planning in relation to individual children's needs and experiences. These, together with their records of children's development, will enable them to plan more effectively for the next stage of learning.

   The staff involvement can also be monitored and training needs identified as well as feedback given from an informed position.

KEYS TO GOOD PRACTICE

- Curriculum planning must take place and must be given a high profile in the centre.
- The curriculum should be published in the nursery on the display board.
- All childcare staff should be involved in the curriculum planning, including the students.
- All parents should be involved, particularly if they can contribute something special for all the children.
- All children should be involved. Mutual respect between parent and child can be fostered if together they contribute to the nursery's work.
- Staff should be recognised for the contribution. A curriculum co-ordinator should be identified and, if appropriate, given special training for this important role.
- Children's development should be assessed at intervals agreed with the parents.
- Records should be given to parents and made available to destination schools.
- Care should be taken that the nursery satisfies the Ofsted Inspectors when they visit.

SYSTEMS FOR MANAGING QUALITY ASSURANCE IN EARLY YEARS PROVISION

1

What this chapter covers:
- the pursuit of excellence
- performance indicators and quality assurance
- Total Quality Management.

The pursuit of excellence

The 'pursuit of excellence' was the main concern of all managers at the end of the last century. The movement was led on a popular level by Tom Peters, a charismatic American management theorist.

Peters's work (1987) was based on case studies of the twelve most successful companies in the USA. He wanted to know why they were successful and he discovered that each of them were led by individuals who had six things in common, as listed below.

1 Close to customer market orientation

This is a cliché that some companies have made a way of life. Peters tells the story of how Fritto-Lay has turned a commodity – the humble crisp – into a strongly branded product by the sheer persistence with which its salesmen call on their outlets. Clarks, the West country shoemakers, have a memorable phrase, 'We don't have any marketing eunuchs around here', which sums up their belief that dealing with customers is so important that everyone is involved.

2 Autonomy/entrepreneurship/innovation

Most people are more innovative when the costs of failure – status and self-esteem as much as financial cost – are minimised. True entrepreneurs and entrepreneurial businesses have a particular knack of learning from their failures. In the modern world, companies that cannot learn to live with small failures are never likely to have major successes; but most firms punish failure more thoroughly than they reward success.

3 Hands on, value-driven leadership and integrity

Peters makes a number of points about IBM that show this factor well. First, Tom Watson, the founder, said that his company was built on respect for the individual. Second, that the objective of the company was '. . . to give the customer the best service of any company in the world'. No firm will always meet such high ideals, but if you don't try you won't get close. That it has persuaded its customers to believe its aspirations helps explain why IBM's much slower and more expensive PCs still outsell 'better', cheaper clones in many markets. Another memorable example is the story of the woman who made a mild complaint to Delta Airlines and was delighted to be met at the departure gate by the President of the airline with a personal apology. That *is* leading from the front: demonstrating the values you expect *everyone* in the business to subscribe to.

4 Productivity through people/involvement

People want to belong, to feel ownership – not just in financial terms (although that helps, too). Almost every study to date of management buy-outs has shown that the greater sense of involvement everyone felt as a consequence of the sale has led to productivity gains that were previously thought impossible. The case of National Freight is a classic and well-documented example. Marks & Spencer has a simple rule in its personnel department, 'If you are going to make a mistake with human beings, err on the side of generosity'. Firms that take this view find that people respond accordingly and rarely try to seek undue advantage.

5 Stick to the knitting

Do what you do best and only what you do best unless there are overwhelming reasons to diversify. There is a wealth of evidence that most takeovers fail to meet their objectives and that this is particularly so the further one moves away from the knowledge base of the predator firm.

6 Simple form, lean/loose–tight controls

One of the evergreen issues among management theorists and consultants is getting the balance right between centralisation and decentralisation. The lesson from the successful companies seems to be that this balance can be struck at a variety of points, as long as all concerned are aware of the boundaries. That said, in general: the simpler the organisation structure the better; and, autonomy.'

Peters noted from his observations that managers who had these six things in common spent nearly all their time 'at the coal face' – in the car showroom, the grocery store, the hamburger restaurant or, in our case, the nursery. Peters called this 'managing by walking about' – or 'MBWA'.

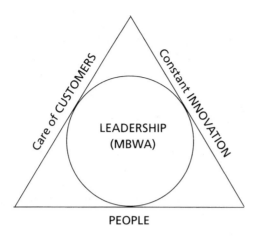

The MBWA triangle

CASE STUDY

'I was recently visiting a newly built corporate nursery in central London as part of a research project and I commented to the manager on what a wonderful space it was. She had a brilliant office sited by the door and so forth and she replied, "Oh, I miss my last nursery. The building was so old that I had to walk through every room to get to my desk. I don't know why but I always felt I had a better handle on things there".'

In the evaluation or monitoring of our work it helps if a system is in place against which standards can be measured while you merely walk about. If these monitoring systems tell you things that surprise you then you are not walking about enough.

For this process the policies and procedures assembled in the nursery portfolio can be used. Of course in the corporate nursery these details will come packaged, and training in their use will have been given by the larger group. However, various methods of monitoring performances exist and are embodied in the National Standards.

Performance indicators

Performance indicators are numerically expressed relationships between one set of data and another that have been identified as a measure of the success, or absence of success, in an organisation, section or unit of an organisation.

They indicate relationships between:

(a) *resources and productivity, e.g.*
  - number of cleaning hours required to keep a nursery to a targeted standard of cleanliness each week
  - number of children being fed each day by a nursery kitchen
  - number of hours lost to a staff team from illness, lateness etc.
  - through-put of a nursery class
(b) *two or more resources, e.g.*
  - full and part-time staff
  - trained and untrained staff
  - professional and support staff
(c) *two or more outcomes, e.g.*
  - percentage attendance at day nursery by age, gender, racial origin
(d) *productivity and potential market, e.g.*
  - percentage of children from outside London attending Great Ormond Street Hospital.

Performance indicators are based upon two sets of comparisons:
(a) comparison of relationship between two or more factors (see above)
(b) comparison between:
  - performance indicators in one centre over time, i.e. June 2003 to June 2004
  - performance indicators and externally or internally set targets, and
  - performance indicators between two or more centres, e.g. percentage of staff illness in Centre A compared with Centre B over the same time period.

For any of these comparisons, the use of *only one* indicator will distort the result. Consider the examples given above and identify the other indicators necessary to reduce distortion. For example, the relative employment of full- and part-time staff may depend more upon the number of appropriately trained people applying for employment within these categories than perseverance with policy targets.

Unfortunately, the media and authorities often focus upon single indicators and base judgements, planning or resource decisions upon them. These are then likely to be inaccurate, or unjust. It is necessary to understand that indicators *indicate*; they do not *direct*.

Origin of requirements
Requirements for performance indicators often come from outside the organisation, usually from resourcing authorities, e.g. Ofsted. There may be a chain of demands: national demanding regional; regional requiring local; local requiring from single units or organisations, and so on.

They may also be used for internal reviewing and evaluation, resource deployment and quality assurance. There is a strong argument for small nurseries to set their own performance indicators and then to discuss these within their small teams or resource authorities, rather than, or as well as, waiting until figures are requested from the Ofsted inspectorate.

There is evidence to show that where indicators are designed, and 'owned' by people at operational levels, they are likely to be more accurate and less resented.

Quality of information

The 'garbage in, garbage out' principle applies, i.e. the aid to judgement these indicators provide depends upon the employment of accurate and reliable information. Where indicators are required by an external and higher authority, those who prepare them may fudge them in order to:
- defend their jobs, organisation, resources, status, reputation and/or
- present a case for more resources.

Information inputs may also be unreliable because:
- they are not considered by staff to be of sufficiently high priority, when compared with 'getting on with the job', i.e. looking after the children
- they are required from professionals who resent this intrusion upon their perception of their specialist roles
- they are obtained from personnel who are too distant from the activity being measured and therefore can misinterpret data
- there is no mechanism for checking mistakes.

Collection cycles and time lag

Collection of complex data may take a considerable length of time. It is also common that data will only be completed at the end of the exercise, or at the end of a given time period, for example, at the end of a financial year. Performance indicators offer a powerful aid to planning and resource decision-making but when there has been such a delay, this is limited by changes that may have taken place during the time lag. For example, decisions for the coming year may need to be made based upon indicators from the year before last, if those from the previous year are still being processed. Short collection cycles are therefore recommended. These offer opportunities for speedier corrective or regulating action but obviously it requires more resources to increase their frequency.

Cost of performance indicators

Recording, collecting and processing information for performance indicators involves resource costs. Opponents of their use argue that cost of their production may equal the resource savings resulting from more informed decisions.

Means are available to reduce costs, such as:
- sampling, i.e. collection of information from representative examples
- computerising the processing, which should also reduce the time lag
- integrating the recording with routine activities, which is the system recommended in a early years context.

Hard and soft indicators

Hard performance indicators are based upon comparatively objective information – for example, number of people resident in an institution over a year; average stay in a postnatal ward.

Soft performance indicators attempt to measure less quantifiable and/or more subjective factors – for example, public reputation and quality of service. This cannot be measured in the same way as hard indicators and usually relies upon client/customer judgement, often using interviews or questionnaires.

A 'harder' ingredient can be introduced in measuring such success factors – for example, by recording the number of people recommended by friends, and the amount of repeat business. Soft indicators should not – for all their difficulties – be neglected; it can be argued that their significance to decision-makers in judging the successful performance of an organisation equals that provided by hard indicators.

In the nursery

Evaluation of the work should be undertaken regularly at a time set in advance. This should include reviewing what the systems are, revealing how easy they are to use and how easy it is to retrieve useful data. Use relevant nursery documentation.

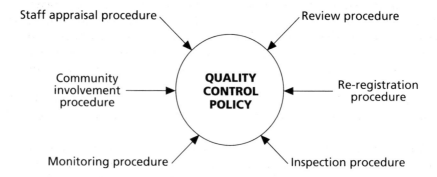

Procedures underpinned by quality control policy

Total Quality Management (TQM)

Total quality management (TQM) is a quality-assurance technique that was developed in the late 1970s in response to the gradual acceptance of the idea that change was becoming commonplace in most organisations.

TQM was adopted in businesses, e.g. British Telecom in the early 1980s, to encourage continuous improvement in every aspect of the work of the organisation. TQM is based on the assumption that continual striving to reach higher and higher standards in every part of the organisation will provide a series of small improvements that will add up to superior performance. Such efforts point in the right direction, towards organisations able to learn and adapt to the needs of a rapidly changing environment. TQM does not entail dramatic changes in structure and systems – more of a continuous fine-tuning than a sudden and complete overhaul.

TQM claims that if things are written down and put into some sort of routine (are systemised) then the quality of the work can be maintained throughout the ups and downs of everyday events and inevitable minor crises.

Here, again, there is no research work from childcare settings – although our own professional intelligence (and several sad incidents in the field) are testament to the fact that if routines are not observed and systems are not laid down, bad practice follows and the children suffer. It had not been the tradition in nurseries to enforce TQM and so this became long overdue. The National Standards became law in September 2001 and provide a good tool for the purpose.

TQM can easily be brought into nurseries and childcare settings using the standards and the 1989 Children Act, the policies it requires and the procedures developed from these – see Chapter 3.

From each one of the four policies and fourteen standards, procedures can be devised. (As discussed in Chapter 3, a policy is a collective agreed statement of beliefs. Procedures are the practices by which the policies are implemented in the nursery – the way of doing things. The procedures are underpinned by the policies.) For example, a simple checklist can be devised for all nursery systems, checks can be undertaken at a set time, can be recorded and signed for. Displays can be checked routinely, recorded and signed for.

All books, incidents/accidents can be routinely checked, recorded and signed for. First aid/fire equipment can be checked, recorded and signed for.

Children's records can be reviewed routinely by key workers, recorded and signed for. Each nursery unit within the nursery should devise its own quality assurance systems using whatever method is most sympathetic to their own individual situation.

Activity

This activity is designed to develop skills in quality assurance. Check whether you have copies of the following policies in the centre in which you work. Copy the list below, tick as appropriate and attach copies of the policies to this list.

	Attached	Not available
Curriculum/Language		
Parents as Partners		
Equal Opportunities		
Health and Safety		
Child Protection		
Admissions		
Food Management		
Behaviour Management		
Staffing (including support staff)		
Volunteers		
Outings for Children		
Settling In		
Other (please specify)		

Where your centre does not have current policies, begin work on collecting the information that you require to draw them up before the next inspection is upon you.

KEYS TO GOOD PRACTICE

- Ensure a prodecure is in place to check and sign for all systems:
  - staffing
  - safety
  - children's records
  - Ofsted proceses
  - resources
  - finances
  - marketing
  - curriculum
  - external relations.
- Set aside one day each term (or period as appropriate) to check that the systems are not telling you things you don't know already.

CONCLUSION

In concluding this book on good practice, we feel it is important to include a short postscript concerned with good practice in developing your own style and helping you towards a quiet assurance in your own work by adopting a few tactics.

As we have already discussed, there is no single right way of being an effective manager. However, there are many wrong ways. By including some or all of the following suggestions in your own management style, you are far more likely to become that effective manager, whilst – at the same time – also developing strategies for coping with your life outside work.

GOOD PRACTICE POINTS

- **Do not brood over things. Talk over your worry, everyone needs to do this at different times in their life.** Choose a friend, relative or professional helper you can trust – avoid choosing a member of staff in your own organisation.

Some results: You will have relief from strain and be more able to see what you can do about your problem.

- **Do not spend all your time on one issue. Escape from your problem, even if only for a while.** Lose yourself for a while in a change of scene, or an interest. There is no merit in 'sticking it out' and suffering.

Some results: Afterwards, you will be clearer-headed to come back and tackle your problem.

- **Being angry is allowed and even healthy. Use up anger by physical activity.** Channel your anger into a job that needs doing, clean out a cupboard or scrub a floor, or take a long walk or play a physical game.

Some results: You will 'let go' of your anger instead of bottling it up, which causes more tension.

- **Do not always insist on getting your own way.** Give in to others occasionally. This is easier on your nervous system in the long-run and you are the one who counts.

Some results: You will feel a relief from pressure and develop a stronger sense of maturity.

- **Be generous with your time and praise. Do something for someone else.** Even a smile or a generous word is a good start. Add to this daily.

Some results: It will help you to feel less isolated with your worry and to start to turn your thoughts outwards.

- **Do not take on everything at once. Deal with one thing at a time.** Select the urgent tasks first and get on with them; forget the rest for the time being. Tension and worry makes even an ordinary day seem unbearable. This need not be a permanent state.

Some results: This will help you to achieve something and the other tasks will seem easier when you get around to them.

- **Do not expect too much from staff or yourself. Try not to be a perfectionist in everything.** If you expect too much of yourself all the time you can create a constant state of worry and anxiety. So decide which things you do well and put your major effort into these first.

Some results: You will avoid an open invitation to yourself to fail, and probably make life easier for yourself, and others.

- **Do not adopt a judgemental approach to things. Try not to be too critical of others – or yourself.** Concentrate on other people's and your own good points and try to understand and develop them.

Some results: You will feel less frustrated and let down by yourself and others.

- **Invest energy in team building. Develop co-operation with others, not competition.** Give the other person a chance. If you are no longer a threat to that person, he or she stops being a threat to you.

Some results: You will have less emotional or physical tension over reaching goals – real or imaginary.

- **If someone is upset, do not stand on your dignity. Make yourself available to others – make the first move occasionally.** Neither push too much nor withdraw too much. Feelings of rejection and neglect are very painful but are often self-imposed.

Some results: At least you will know you have made an effort and this will build your confidence.

- **Make the most of your private life. Plan your recreation time, however short.** Allow some time for a hobby or recreation. Unplanned time often becomes wasted time. Make variety part of the planning.

Some results: You will return to your work, or your problem, with a fresher outlook.

- **If you are continually stressed, get some help – do not just suffer. Learn methods of exercise and relaxation and practice them daily.** You are aiming to be in control of your body and learning how to counteract tension and anxiety.

Some results: You will unlock tension in every part of your body and even prevent tension in the future.

APPENDIX: REFERENCES

Belbin, R.M., 1981. *Management Teams. Why they Succeed or Fail*, Butterworth Heinemann, Guildford.

Bruce, T., 1987. *Early Childhood Education*, Hodder & Stoughton, London.

Department for Education and Skills, 2001. *Special Educational Needs Code of Practice*.

Department for Education and Skills with QCA, 2000. *Curriculum Guidance for the Foundation Stage*.

Fielder, F.E., 1972. Validation and Extension of the Contingency Model of Leadership Effectiveness, *Psychological Bulletin*, **76,** 128–48.

Handy, C., 1986. *Understanding Organisations, Penguin, London.*

Handy, C., 1989. *The Age of Unreason*, Business Books Ltd, London.

Handy, C., 1992. *The Gods of Management,* Penguin, London.

Harrison, R., 1972. How to Describe your Organization, *Harvard Business Review*, Sept/Oct 1972.

Herzberg, F., 1966. *Work and the Nature of Man,* World Publishing Co., New York.

Herzberg, F., 1968. One More Time: How do you Motivate Employees?, *Harvard Business Review,* **46**.

Holmes, F.H. and Rahe, R. H., 1967. The Social Readjustment Rating Scale, *Journal of Psychomatic Research,* **11,** 213–18.

Jones, A. and Bitton, K., 1992. *The Future Shape of Children's Services*, National Children's Bureau, London.

Levinson, Daniel J., 1978. *The Seasons of a Man's Life,* Ballantine Books, New York.

Maslow, A., 1954. *Motivation and Personality,* Harper & Row, New York.

Moss, P. and Pearce, A., 1995. *Valuing Quality in Early Childhood Services*, Paul Chapman, London.

Peters, T., 1987. *Thriving on Chaos – A Handbook for Management Revolution*, Macmillan Ltd, London.

Peters, T. and Waterman, R. H., 1982. *In Search of Excellence,* Harper & Row, New York.

Rodd, J., 1994. *Leadership in Early Childhood*, OUP, Oxford.

Rosenthal, R. and Jacobson, L., 1968. *Pygmalion in the Classroom,* Holt, Rinehart & Winston, New York.

Rotter, J.B., 1966. Generalised Expectancies for Internal versus External Control of Reinforcement, *Psychological Monographs,* **30,** 1–26.

Selye, H., 1956. *The Stress of Life,* McGraw Hill, New York.

Further reading

Audit Commission, 1994. *Seen but not Heard. Co-ordinating Community Child Health and Social Services for Children in Need*, HMSO, London.

Bone, M., 1977. *Pre-school Children and the Need for Daycare: OPCS Social Survey*, HMSO, London.

Clutterbuck, D., 1985. *Everyone Needs a Mentor,* Institute of Personnel Management, London.

Cohen, P., 1992. *A New Deal for Children? Implementation of the Children Act 1989 in the Counties*, Association of County Councils Publications, London.

Department of Health, 1993. *Children's Daycare Facilities at 31st March 1992*, HMSO, London.

Department of Health, 1989. *The Children Act 1959: Guidance and Regulations. Volume 2: Family Support, Daycare and Educational Provision for Young Children,* HMSO, London.

Department for Education and Skills, 2003 *The Effective Provision of Pre-School Education (EPPE) Project.*

Drucker P. 1973. *Management,* Harper & Row, New York.

Elfer, P., 1991. The Children Act and Daycare, *National Children's Bureau Guidelines, No. 100,* London.

National Children's Bureau, 1994. *Young Children in Group Daycare: Guidelines for Good Practice,* NCB, London.

Ofsted, 2001. *Full Daycare – Guidance to the National Standards,* HMSO.

OPCS, 1995. *Daycare Services for Children,* HMSO, London.

Pugh, G., 1988. *Services for Under Fives,* National Children's Bureau, London.

Pugh, G., 1992. *Contemporary Issues in the Early Years,* Paul Chapman/National Children's Bureau, London.

Pugh, G., 1993. *30 Years of Change for Children,* National Children's Bureau, London.

Rubin, Z. and McNeil, E.B., 1983. *The Psychology of Being Human,* Harper & Row, London.

Schaffer, R.H., 1990. *Making Decisions about Children: Psychological Questions and Answers,* Basil Blackwell, Oxford.

Smith, P., 1989. Overview of the Children Act 1989, *National Children's Bureau Guidelines, No. 91,* London.

Stott, K. and Walker, A., 1992. *Making Management Work,* Prentice Hall, New York.

Sure Start, 2003. *Birth to Three Matters – a Framework to Support Children in their Earliest Years.*

Thomas Coram Research Unit, 1994. *Implementing the Children Act for Children under Eight,* HMSO, London.

Wandsworth Council, 2003. *Planning for Foundation Stage Learning.*

INDEX